PREPOLOGY 101

BY CHRIS KOHOUT

www.prepologyHQ.com

Give feedback on the book at:
chris@prepologyHQ.com

First Edition - Printed in the U.S.A.

Dedication

To my amazing wife, Jennifer. The family we've made together is the most important thing in my world.

Table Of Contents

WHY I WROTE THIS

The best preparation for good work tomorrow
is to do good work today. —Elbert Hubbard

Let's try something new, shall we?

Prepping is a big deal these days. A growing number of television shows have capitalized on the idea of preparedness. Sadly, they've also drawn a caricature image of paranoid fanatics with a loose grasp on reality. Other shows like The Walking Dead have romanticized the thought of post-apocalyptic survival. And don't get me started on the vast ocean of content available on the internet.

In short, there's a lot of prepper info out there.

But that's a problem in itself. Who has the time and energy to sort through the myriad resources out there, studying, comparing and separating the wheat from the BS? Apparently, I did.

As both a programmer and a writer, I enjoy diving into vast, complex systems. The enjoyment comes from bringing order out of chaos. Admittedly, being a parent of young children inspires additional incentive. At some point, I stopped and realized just how much data I had plowed through, and figured it didn't make sense for that much labor to benefit only myself. With a bit more effort, I could distill my discoveries into a form that others could use as a massive time-saver.

So here we are.

Warning: Not all preps are sexy

As it's always been, our world is a chaotic, wonderful, frightening, glorious place to live. We can never know what life has planned for us. If we did, what would be the point of living? But that uncertainty sometimes exacts a sharp price. It only makes sense that we seek to minimize our risk.

There are many things to fear, and it's not my place to tell anyone their choices are wrong. But, none of us are blessed with an infinite amount of time or resources. We simply can't afford to cover all the bases. The list of all possible threats, and possible counters to them, is just too much.

Instead, I advocate for the idea of prepping for the most common threats first. After all, by definition, they are the ones most likely to befall us. What that list contains is different for us all. It depends on who you are, the life you lead, and where you live it.

If your family lives on the Florida coast, you face different threats than someone living alone in New Mexico. If you've neglected your health for the past decade, then you have a different risk portfolio than someone who maintains a good level of fitness.

Granted, some risks are sexier than others. I saw a funny poster at the game development studio I used to work at: "The hardest part of the zombie apocalypse will be pretending it's not freaking awesome."

Hey, I love The Walking Dead as much as the next guy. Living by my wits, combating the living dead by rifle and machete? Hell, yeah. Sign me up!

I'd much rather go to the range and practice long-range shooting than go run a few miles. But, I also know that I'm not getting any younger, and the insidious effects of age are far more likely to impact my life than a slavering zombie. So... I sigh, and go run. Sometimes prepping isn't fun.

It's important to monitor yourself, and be honest about your motivations for prepping. Why? Because if you fall into the trap of only focusing on the sexy preps, you'll be doing yourself and your loved ones a disservice. You will have fooled yourself into feeling prepared when you're not. And I don't think anyone reading this book feels that's a good place to be.

What to expect

I'm not a doomsday evangelist. My reasons for writing this book do not include the following:

» The end of the world as we know it (TEOTWAWKI)

» Catastrophic collapse of the American economy

» Killer asteroids

» Zombie hordes

Are those things within the realm of possibility? Sure, nearly anything is possible. But I'd rather put my precious time, money and energy into enjoying my life. For me, that means being prepared for the things more likely to affect me and mine, and then drawing comfort from that work. Even if you do choose to prepare for more extreme possibilities, it still makes sense to tackle the more likely ones first, right? Preparedness brings peace of mind. The point is to enjoy life, not let paranoia run rampant. I prefer a mindful, measured approach to risk-assessment. A fearful attitude about the future sucks the joy from the present.

OK, that said, let's get to it!

WHY NOT FEMA?

After Katrina, most people have heard of FEMA, and not typically in a favorable sense. I don't want to wade into political/conspiratorial waters, but given that they are the federal entity tasked with emergencies, it's worth hitting the basics.

If there's a well-funded ($10 billion) federal agency in charge of such things, doesn't that mean we're all good? Maybe this whole prepping thing is unnecessary? Well, let's take a look.

In 1978, President Jimmy Carter signed Executive Order 12127, which took many different government agencies and merged them into the Federal Emergency Management Agency. At first, they had twin missions: natural disaster preparedness and civil defense. Remember, the cold war was still a thing back then.

The new organization responded to the dumping of toxic waste into Love Canal in Niagara Falls, NY in the late 1970s. They also handled the Three Mile Island nuclear accident. During the 1990s, as the Soviet Union became less of a threat to national security, FEMA's twin responsibilities were streamlined into just one: natural disasters.

Over the years, Congress added more and more responsibilities to the agency, with ever-increasing budgets to match. Then, after the 1995 sarin gas attack on the Tokyo subway, FEMA was also given authority for counter terrorism. Following the September 11, 2001 attacks, Congress created the Department of Homeland Security, which absorbed FEMA within it. This shift away from its traditional focus on natural disasters caused an exodus of experienced staffers.

President Bush appointed Michael Brown as FEMA's director in 2003, a role he had little experience in. Brown soon warned that FEMA's absorption into DHS would "fundamentally sever FEMA from its core functions", "shatter agency morale" and "break longstanding, effective and tested relationships with states and first responder stakeholders".

He warned the inevitable result of the reorganization would be "an ineffective and uncoordinated response" to a terrorist attack or a natural disaster. Two years later, hurricane Katrina would make his words seem prophetic, although his emails during the emergency now paint a damning picture of his command of the situation.

In his last extended TV interview on CNN, Brown admitted that the federal government did not know that thousands of survivors without food or water had taken shelter at the city's convention center, despite a day of news reports.

Bruce P. Baughman, Alabama emergency management director, head of the National Emergency Management Association and the official in charge of FEMA's response to the World Trade Center and Pentagon attacks in 2001, said Katrina will leave its mark on federal disaster management. "It's time to realize, whoever is in charge of FEMA does need an emergency management background. . . . It's something you learn by experience, and a lot of that experience is gone," he said.

Michael Brown no longer works in the public sector, and currently hosts a radio talk show on 630 KHOW in Denver, Colorado.

When Congress appointed a bipartisan committee to investigate FEMA's failures, they reported: "For years emergency management professionals have been warning that FEMA's preparedness has eroded. Many believe this erosion is a result of the separation of the preparedness function from FEMA, the drain of long-term professional staff along with their institutional knowledge and expertise, and the inadequate readiness of FEMA's national emergency response teams. The combination of these staffing, training, and organizational structures made FEMA's inadequate performance in the face of a disaster the size of Katrina all but inevitable."

The Bottom Line

At times, FEMA has been a professional, effective, lifesaving entity. At other points in its history, it has failed terribly. While I'm glad such an agency exists, I choose not to rely on them for myself or my family.

STAY OR GO?

One of the biggest challenges you'll face is whether it's better to hunker down and bug in at home, or leave home behind and head to a remote location. This single question is tough because so much rides on your answer. Pulling your family away from a familiar support system will be stressful and possibly dangerous. But is staying any better?

The time to think through such issues is now, while you can remain calm and use logic, not emotion, to reach a decision. Sure, you can't prejudge every possible situation, but you can evaluate under what future circumstances you will stay, and which ones will compel you to leave.

There is no single right answer to this dilemma, because it can't be answered without taking into account three things:

1) The nature of the emergency

Is the event one that will likely put you in physical danger? For example, an impending hurricane, fire or flood, where there's a good chance of injury if you remain. Or is it one that can be weathered with proper planning, like an ice storm that knocks out electricity for two weeks?

Think about the possible threats in your area, and judge which of them constitutes a threat to your safety, regardless of how well prepared you are. In those situations, the right choice is probably to leave.

2) Your family's ability to bug out.

If you're single, fit, and have a positive attitude, then your ability to bug out may be good. But what if you have a family with young children? Maybe you're caring for an older parent? Perhaps the idea of camping gives your spouse the willies. In those cases, you'll need to be honest about assessing your ability to leave the comfort of home.

3) Bugging out vs. Evacuating

This is a critical distinction that often gets overlooked. When people plan and assemble their bugout bag, the assumption is usually that there're prepping to live in the wilderness. That's certainly the

Think long and hard before leaving the comfort and security of your home.

romantic view. Take to the hills! Live off the land! I'll discuss that more in a bit.

If you decide leaving home is the best course of action, then what are your options for a safe landing place? It is always preferable to evacuate to a known destination like a distant relative's home, than to head for the mountains. If you haven't already, speak to them now and ensure they will take you in. It may not be possible to contact them when something happens.

Your options, from best to worst:

Bug In

My first choice is always to hunker down and bug in. Consider some of the advantages:

» You know the immediate area intimately well

» You know the surrounding area

» You have a ready stock of supplies

» You are in a familiar environment, which counts for a lot in an emergency

» You know the people around you

» Your neighbors have a vested interest in getting through this, which leads to cooperation

» You avoid the dangers of travel, such as downed power lines, broken roads, desperate people, or running out of food/water

» The time and energy it takes to travel can instead be spent on getting your home set up and comfortable

These are just some of the benefits you receive by simply staying put. Unless the situation really forced my hand, I'd settle in and take advantage of all the preps I have already set in place.

But if that's not possible? If a raging fire threatened to engulf my house? Well, time to implement Plan B...

Evacuation

My second choice, if I'm forced to leave, is to leave for a known location, via a known route.

We already have an agreement with a close relative 90 minutes away. At any time, if need be, we are welcome. So if things come to that, I don't have to worry about establishing communication and seeking permission. It's already given. I just need to get there safely.

To that end, I have my evacuation bag packed and ready to be thrown into the car. It's a large duffel-style bag, filled with a good supply of everything my family will need, both for survival and comfort.

It is NOT a bugout bag. For one thing, it's way too big to haul on my back for any real distance. Fully loaded, it comes in at around 70 pounds, but that's ok. It's meant to be used for evacuation, which means we're driving. Another difference between it and a BOB is that it's not focused on wilderness survival. Being able to make some assumptions about where we're going means I can devote space to things we'll need, while avoiding those we won't.

As part of my evacuation plans, I've mapped out several routes, in case my primary road is inaccessible. I also have enough fuel stocked to get there. So even if Murphy really bites us, and something happens just when the car happens to be low on gas, I know we can still make it.

Bug Out

As an absolute last resort, I do have a bug out bag. It's a rugged yet comfortable backpack, stocked with the gear and supplies I'd need to get me to a safer location. Since it is designed to be carried, I keep the total weight down to around 25 pounds, which is light enough for long hikes. It is very easy to go crazy and load up a bag, but all that gear won't help you much if you're struggling to haul it after two miles.

I know most people stock their BOB, then leave it alone, but I like to practice with mine. I think of it more as my bushcraft bag, really. If you're not familiar with that term, it just means being able to move and survive comfortably through the wilderness with a minimum of gear. I go into detail and bushcraft later.

Personally, I think it's extremely valuable to put your preps into practice. Many things don't work the way you think they will, and it's way better to find out the issues now, rather than learning them too late when you're actually depending on them.

A bugout bag contains everything you need to get from point A to point B.

Most weekends, we take the kids out for a hike somewhere, often to check out a cool waterfall. While these are relatively easy hikes, it's still great practice for me. I always wear my BOB, so I've gotten acclimated to it. I know what it feels like to haul it through the woods, and I've made little adjustments to it over time, to make things more comfortable. I've learned more about how to pack things better, and which gear I need, and which sounded good, but turned out to be unneeded.

Bottom Line

Think about your possible threats now, and how you want to respond to them. Have an evacuation site planned. Take advantage of your home, for as long as you can.

LAYERS OF PREP

Once you start diving into the prepping world, things can quickly seem overwhelming. There's just too much information to take in. The internet brings a tsunami of ideas, advice, warnings and buying options. It's easy to feel your head's underwater from the onslaught.

One way to combat that feeling is to have a framework in mind, or a system that helps organize everything. By breaking it all down into manageable chunks, you can get your arms around it and start making progress toward your goals. I like to think of it in layers, beginning with the mind, then working outward, like this:

» Attitude/Knowledge/Skills

» Body/Clothing

» Vehicle

» Home

» Finances

» Community

By thinking about what needs you have at each layer, it helps make sense of the flood of information.

Skills

Skills are the ultimate prep. Once you have them, they're with you anytime, anywhere. Did the smoke alarm go off at 3AM, forcing you to get everyone out safely? You might still be in your underwear, but you've got your skills.

Skills also don't weigh anything. In bushcraft, it's a truism that the more you know, the less gear you need. The lighter your pack is, the farther you can go.

Skills also have a way of instilling confidence and opening your world to new experiences and realities you never noticed before. After learning how easy it is to get a fire started with birch bark, you'll find yourself noticing birches as you hike along. Knowledge feels good.

Medical

One of the best skill sets to work on is medical training. While most of us will never be able to invest the time and money into a full medical degree, that's ok. There are still a range of medical abilities available to learn, and even a basic course will give you a solid grounding to deal with many situations.

I recommend **Solo Schools** (http://soloschools.com) for medical coursework. They offer a great variety of courses, and are available as home courses, or hands-on programs all over the country.

Some of the certificates you can earn:

Wilderness First Aid - The WFA is the perfect course for the outdoor enthusiast or trip leader who wants a basic level of first aid training for short trips with family, friends, and outdoor groups. The WFA is 16 hours long (two days), and focuses on the basic skills of: Response and Assessment, Musculoskeletal Injuries, Environmental Emergencies, Survival Skills, Soft Tissue Injuries, and Medical Emergencies.

Wilderness First Aid Afloat - Covers the same material at the WFA, but also includes additional topics that are of specific interest to boaters, such as sea sickness, marine bites and stings, and some types of injuries that are more common in marine environments.

Wilderness First Responder - The WFR is the perfect course for anyone working in a position of leadership in an outdoor setting or for individuals who want a high level of wilderness medical training for extended personal backcountry trips or expeditions. The WFR is 72-80 hours long (7 to 10 days), and is a comprehensive and in-depth look at the standards and skills of dealing with: Response and Assessment, Musculoskeletal Injuries, Environmental Emergencies and Survival Skills, Soft Tissue Injuries, and Medical Emergencies. Although these appear to be the same basic topics covered in the two-day WFA course, they are covered far more extensively, and there is much more hands-on practice.

Medical training is an excellent investment in your skillset.

Wilderness Emergency Medical Technician - The WEMT is designed for people who work, or plan to work, as professional medical personnel on fire departments, rescue squads, and ambulance crews, especially those working far from definitive care (e.g. on rural or wilderness rescue teams). The WEMT is 170+ hours long (typically taught in 20 days, spread out over four weeks, with weekends off), and combines the standard Department of Transportation Emergency (DOT) Medical Technician curriculum with wilderness-specific medical training that focuses on long-term care (our WFR curriculum).

Search and Rescue - Topics range from classic SAR training, to orienteering (map and compass), to winter survival skills, to bivouac and shelter building.

Off road driving

So you've bought that perfect 4X4 as your bugout vehicle, but do you really know the right way to handle it off road? Or the proper techniques to recover it once you get stuck? Or what recovery gear you should be carrying? There's only so much you can learn from books and Youtube. At some point, you'll want real, hands-on instruction and practice.

Check out **Overland Experts** (http://overlandexperts.com), for an example of the instruction they provide. As CEP Bruce Elfstrom says, "You will see no power point presentations here, nor some static shop covering field repairs. OEX is nothing but field orientated, pragmatic, realistic and modest in its approach. We know that a combination of hands on training and repetition, lecture and attention to differing learning styles is the key to a long lasting and reliable skill set."

Firearms

Prepping and shooting seem to go together like chocolate and peanut butter. If you're going to own firearms, learn how to handle and care for them responsibly. A Google search should find you plenty of local options, but http://training.nra.org is also a good starting point.

Hunting

While I don't recommend the idea of living off the land as practical in a true emergency situation, knowing how to effectively take and process an animal is a fantastic skill to have.

First step, get your hunters safety certification. Check Google for your state's options. The archives of http://fieldandstream.com are a wealth of information. Think about joining a local hunting association, and finding an experienced hunter to take you under their wing.

Bushcraft

Bushcraft, or wilderness skills, is growing quickly in popularity and is a welcoming community for beginners. Learning the basics of fire building, shelters, fishing, water purification, hunting, trapping, and wilderness cooking can go a long way in preparing you for a wide variety of situations.

http://BushcraftUSA.com is a great resource to learn from others, ask questions, swap gear reviews, or meet people in your area who want to get out into the woods and practice their skills. With a little perseverance, I found some great local guys to meet up with. Now we have monthly get-togethers with our families, where we work on skills, cook lunch over the fire, and explore nearby woods for edible flora.

Of particular interest is the at-home bushcraft certification. Volunteers have created a series of Youtube videos that demonstrate various skills. You watch them, then perform the same skill yourself, and submit a picture or video for verification.

If you're not sure how to get started with learning wilderness skills, this offers a fantastic, free structure to follow. Certifications are available for Basic, Intermediate and Advanced skills. Once you've

created an account, you'll find the certification steps here: http://
bushcraftusa.com/forum/showthread.php/27234-Bushclass-Index

Another great way to learn these skills is through watching them in
action. Here are some of my favorite Youtube channels:

AlfieAesthetics - Lots of wry
humor, and deep knowledge of
flora.

Survival Lilly - From Austria,
Lilly demonstrates hunting,
shelter building, and much more.

Armouredcockroach - British
ex-military gent who tours the area in his kitted-out 4x4.

BlackOwlOutdoors - Stylishly shot gear reviews and skill demos.

Darkorian321 - A collection of older Ray Mears (a bushcraft legend)
videos. Fantastic stuff.

Iawoodsman - Lots of skill demos. Also one of the admins from
bushcraftusa.com.

MCQBushcraft - Probably my favorite. Mike is a professional
bushcraft instructor, and he's a pleasure to watch.

Taromovies - Great cold-climate outings. He makes it all look easy!

ZedOutdoors - Zed chronicles his own progress, plus interviews
many interesting folks along the way.

Prepping Your Leadership

Just like your skills, one of the things you know you'll always have
with you is your attitude. How you choose to see the world around
you matters tremendously, whether you're interviewing for a job or

managing a scared, tired group during a crisis.

This outlook is continuously being transmitted to those around you, especially in times of stress. Your family will be looking to you not just for direction, but for clues as to how worried they should be. Your mental state will give rise to signals that those around will pick up. And those signals will turn into either fruitful action or panicked despair.

As much as possible, I look for actual, historical events for guidance in matters of prepping. In the case of leadership, and the effect that both good and bad examples have on a group, history provides an amazing example.

Our illustrative story takes place in 1864, in the rough, desolate southern ocean between Antarctica and New Zealand. A small crew of only five men sailed aboard the Grafton, outfitted to explore islands in the area for minerals to make tin. They set sail from Sydney, Australia, planning to spend four months exploring, then to bring back a cargo of the ore. Their search was less than fruitful, and as they approached the Auckland Islands, gale force winds soon buffeted the ship.

Due to tight funding from their investors, their anchor chain was neither long enough not strong enough for the conditions, and they crashed into jagged rocks along the shore. Their ship's bottom was torn asunder. The men all survived, but six months went by with no sign of rescue from the deserted, frozen island.

Incredibly, the universe then played a dark joke, and sent another ship's crew to the same fate, on the other side of the exact same island. This ship, much larger, was the Invercauld, crewed by 25 men.

Neither group ever knew of the other's existence. It would be 12 more long, cold months before both groups would be rescued. But what really makes this story relevant for us is how radically differently the two groups fared.

Both groups survived on the same island at mostly the same time, and yet when rescued, all five members of the Grafton were found alive, with little long-term ill effects. And the 25 man crew of the Invercauld? All but three had perished.

So what made such a dramatic difference in the survivability of the two groups? The leadership and attitudes of each group. After all, the actions taken in the first hours or days of a crisis set the tone for the weeks and months to come. Consider these details:

Grafton

Captain Musgrave encouraged and demonstrated an optimistic view and strove to get the most utility from each man.

» Upon crashing, the crew stayed with the ship until morning, so they could salvage usable items from the wreckage.

» Emergency shelter was quickly set up for everyone.

» Musgrave called for an election of leadership, realizing that their previous titles meant little now. The men elected him as their leader, and were now willing to contribute and follow orders.

» Remained dedicated to the survival of the entire group.

» Built a 16"x24" shelter with wood walls and thatched with 5000 bundles of grass, complete with stone chimney, a wood floor and windows salvaged from the wreck.

» Unraveled sail cloth and spun it into new thread.

» Hunted seals and other animals with a salvaged gun.

» Once they decided to try to build a boat to escape, they built a blacksmith forge and made 700 nails, bolts, saw blades and other tools.

» Salted and smoked excess meat to preserve it for future times.

» Started a school in the evenings, since they realized each man knew something the others did not. This helped develop bonds and camaraderie among the men.

Invercauld

Captain Dalgarno made little effort to lead his men, and was frequently despondent. Despite their new circumstances, he continued to act as a ship's captain, treating the other men as his servants.

» Upon crashing, there was no preparation, no call to abandon ship, the ship's three small boats weren't launched, the Captain and officers were shouting impossible and contradictory orders, and a sick young crewman was left on board to drown.

» Not much of the ship's supplies were saved.

» An "every man for himself" attitude prevailed. Crew, such as their cook, were abandoned to die just a few hundred yards from the rest of the group.

» With no sense of unity, the crew split into many factions, each with differing goals.

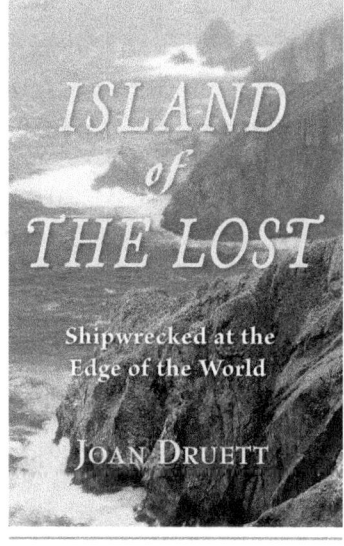

Island Of The Lost tells the full story of the unfortunate crews.

» There were several cases of cannibalism.

» With no leader to drive the men on, even when better circumstances were found, many men instead lied down and died.

» The crew did not trust each other, leading to many sleepless nights.

» As more and more men mimicked the Captain's attitude, apathy and laziness became common.

» While most of the others lie around doing nothing, one lowly seaman explored, built shelter, hunted and found food. Without him, they all would have died.

This true story of leadership and survival holds crucial lessons for anyone preparing themselves and their family for an emergency situation. Effective leaders remain committed to the welfare of those they lead, and drive the group forward, even when all seems lost.

Prepping Your Body

Think about this: your body is the ultimate bug out vehicle. It runs on a wide variety of fuels, can handle wildly varied terrain, and contains multiple environmental sensors. If that isn't enough, it can even repair itself. No Jeep Wrangler can match that.

So it makes sense to ensure it's kept in good working order. I've seen a lot of folks who stock their car with enough supplies to cross the country on a moment's notice, but they themselves couldn't run a mile if their life depended on it. That's not just laziness, that's stupid. You never know when or where something might happen, but you know that when it does, you'll have your body with you. Make it one that can be an asset in tough times.

No man has the right to be an amateur in the matter of physical training. It is a shame for a man to grow old without seeing the beauty and strength of which his body is capable.

— Socrates

Whether you think the shit is going to hit the fan any day now, or you just want to make sure you're around to see your kids get married, it just makes sense to maintain a good level of fitness. I know, it's too easy to overeat in our country. And there's no shortage of people selling you easy fitness. Here's the one simple truth to remember: there is no silver bullet.

For some fortunate few, working out is fun. My brother has that particular freakishness. I do not. For me, it's never really fun, but I try to keep up with it anyway. But I also don't handicap my efforts by believing the BS that progress can come easily. It's simple (but not easy): eat clean and work hard.

Want a plan to follow? Check out Crossfit. I've been doing it for six months, and I admit, it's an ass kicker. It will definitely show you where you're weak. But the camaraderie is fantastic. You're there struggling with others, and supporting each other's victories. It's particularly well suited for prepping, since the exercises are all very "real world" based activities. Running, jumping, hauling heavy things. It just makes you a better you.

Nutrition

As they like to say at my Crossfit gym, "you can't out-train a bad diet". It's tempting to justify that double cheeseburger by hitting the track for a mile or two, but if you do, you need to run the numbers again. A Whopper with cheese comes in at 730 calories. Say you run two miles at a 12 minute mile pace. Congrats, you burned off 300 calories. Now keep going for another 35 minutes, and you'll break even. That's a lot of running to just end up where you started.

The solution? Develop a taste for less calorically-dense foods: fruits and vegetables. I'm still working on this one, myself. Easier said than done, but good recipe books help. I can improv all sorts of way to prepare a great steak, but when it comes to veggies, I draw a blank. It's nice to follow in someone else's footsteps, and end up with something tasty.

Body Upgrades

While we don't quite have Bionic Man tech (though it seems close), there are still ways to improve your body's abilities. Do you wear glasses or contacts? Look into LASIK surgery. Imagine the freedom of not having to rely on vision aids anymore. In a real emergency, that could be a lifesaver.

How about dental issues? If you have any nagging issues that haven't gotten bad enough yet to visit the dentist, stop procrastinating and get it sorted out now.

Think of it this way: if you knew a serious emergency was one week away, wouldn't you take care of things now?

Every Day Carry (EDC)

Since life is unpredictable, it's wise to think about the very basics that you'd want to have with you at all times. Obviously, you can't go crazy with this, or things become impractical. The idea is to find the right items that easily fit into your current routine, and give you that extra bit of utility when you need it.

What might go in your EDC?

You will probably have your smartphone:

» Address book

» GPS/Maps

» Access to email

» Banking apps

» Family photos

» Internet access

» Kindle app

In addition, you might carry:

» A small multitool

» Cash

» An LED flashlight

» An emergency whistle

» A ferro rod

www.prepologyHQ.com/edc
A shopping list of specific gear for your EDC bag.

Prepping Your Home

"For an Englishman's house is his castle, and each man's home is his safest refuge." — *The Institutes of the Laws of England, by lawyer and politician Sir Edward Coke, 1628.*

Have you tried casing your own house? It's worth the few minutes it takes. Walk outside and have a look from the street. If you wanted to break in, where would you go first? What looks like the easiest entry? How could you make those areas more secure?

Are there places where you'd be hidden from view, in case it takes a few minutes to get inside? Maybe some tall shrubbery in front of the windows, or near the door? Consider trimming those back, and leaving no good hiding spot. Of course, prickly shrubs are nice too.

For best results, do this survey at night. Darkness is comforting to an intruder, so deny it to them. Force them to confront the adversary of light if they want to enter your home. Motion sensing lights are cheap, and offer excellent deterrence.

Doors

Exterior doors should be metal or solid hardwood, and at least 1 3/4 inches thick. Frames must be equally strong. Even the best lock is useless when placed in a weak frame. Replace your door's typically short screws with longer ones, preferably 3 inches.

Look into the various kits available to add steel reinforcement to door frames. These are usually installable within an hour or two.

A peephole is safer to view guests than a door chain.

Do not carry house keys on a key ring bearing your home address. Don't leave house keys with your car in a commercial parking lot or with an attendant. Do not hide your keys in "secret" places outside your home—burglars usually know where to look.

One of the painful things about our time is
that those who feel certainty are stupid,
and those with any imagination and under-
standing are filled with doubt and indecision.
— Bertrand Russell

Windows

3M makes an aftermarket security window film that makes the glass resist break-ins, as well as keeps them from failing under high winds, such as a hurricane.

If possible, store a few sheets of plywood to cover windows in case of extreme weather. Ideally, have them pre-cut to the proper size for your home's windows.

Carbon Monoxide

Carbon monoxide is a colorless, tasteless and odorless compound produced by incomplete combustion of carbon containing materials. It is often referred to as the "silent killer" because it is virtually undetectable without using detection technology and most do not realize they are being poisoned.

It's particularly scary in an emergency situation, because the types of things people are tempted to do can actually kill them and their family. A lot of people don't realize the lethal danger it poses, so they do things like use propane grills indoors, or run fuel-based heaters in enclosed spaces. Sadly, a quick Google search will turn up many tragic reports of entire households being killed in their sleep due to carbon monoxide poisoning.

Don't take the slightest risk on this. Get a good CO monitor, and swap the batteries in it annually. The monitors are cheap, and do their job well, giving you peace of mind against an enemy you can't see or smell.

Fire

Every home should have multiple fire extinguishers. I like to keep one in the garage, one in the kitchen, and one in our upstairs bedroom.

Be sure to work out egress paths ahead of time. If you all have to evacuate in the middle of the night, what routes will each person take? Where will you meet up?

For upstairs rooms, look into an escape ladder. They are compact and easy to stow under a bed, but can be quickly hooked to a window frame, and dropped down to give you another escape route in case fire has you blocked in.

Dogs

A dog is such a fantastic addition to your home security. With their innate sense of protection, owning a dog is like having extra senses working for you. You'll be aware of visitors sooner. While you're sleeping, you'll have a sentinel on duty, ready to wake you at the sign of trouble. And their bark will discourage those who may think of entering your home unannounced.

Breeds like the German Shepherd, Border Collie, Labs and Rottweilers are excellent. While some breeds have a fearsome or dangerous reputation, I believe that's caused more by the treatment of the animal by the owner.

Vacation Tips

Arrange to have your lawn mowed in summer and your walk and driveway shoveled in winter.

Use automatic timers to turn lights on and off in various parts of the house at appropriate times. Consider connecting a radio to a timer.

Leave blinds open in their usual position.

GET HOME BAG

So we've got your mind, body and home in good shape. If you happen to be home when a disaster strikes, you're prepared to weather the storm.

But what if you're not home? For most of us, commuting to work is a necessary evil. Maybe you live near your work, so a short walk isn't an issue. Or perhaps you're in the suburbs, and face a 30 minute drive back to your safe, well-provisioned home. And if things got bad quickly, even a short distance could be a problem.

It makes sense to think about your plan to get home if you're caught somewhere else during a crisis. That breaks down into two main things to think about: route and supplies.

Route

If the distance involved seems walkable, what route would you take? It almost certainly wouldn't be the same one you'd drive. Fire up Google Maps and map it out. Start at the likely non-home places you might be in, then get walking directions back to your house. See what the distance and estimated time would be. Do they seem realistic? If you're not sure, plan to walk it and see.

Pay attention to places of note along the route. Supermarkets, gas stations and banks would be good to know about. Depending on the situation, you may want to pick up supplies and cash, or you may prefer to avoid those places altogether. Are there railroad tracks along the way? Even if walking them adds some time, it may be worthwhile, to avoid congestion.

Supplies

While driving is preferable, you can't rely on that being possible, so pack supplies in a Get Home Bag that you can take with you on foot.

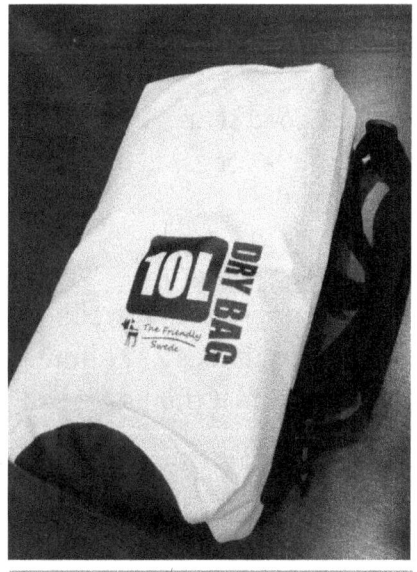

This isn't a bugout bag. It's just to assist in getting you back to home base.

What are some possible hazards you may encounter? And what might you carry to deal with them?

Heat: baseball cap, sunglasses

Cold: warm shirt, spare wool socks, wool cap, emergency bivy, firestarter

Rain: waterproof jacket

Darkness: flashlight

Dry bags are handy containers for a Get Home Bag.

Minor Injury: Altoid medical tin

Getting Lost: map of the area

Hunger/Thirst: emergency food bars, bottled water, sawyer mini filter

Violence: whistle, pepper spray, knife

Other useful items to include: paracord, cash, notepad/pencil, duct tape, multitool.

All of this can be stored in a small waterproof drybag, and kept in the car. I use a 10 liter drybag, with a shoulder strap. It's readily stowable, carries all the basics, and is easy to sling over a shoulder if I'm hoofing it.

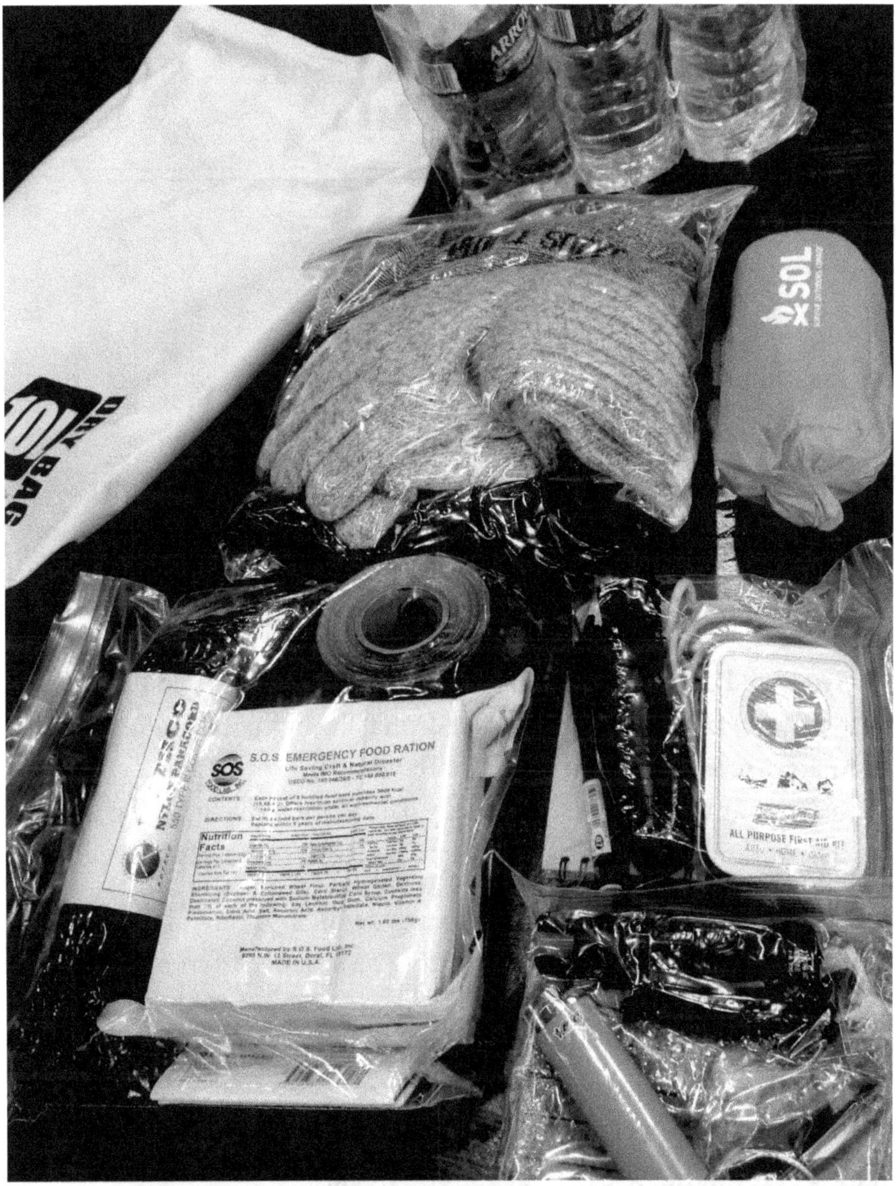

www.prepologyHQ.com/gethomebag
A list of all my gear in my Get Home Bag.

WATER

Assuming you're not in immediate bodily danger, water security is your primary concern.

Humans need a lot of water, and frequently, to remain functional. Water makes up 60% of your total weight, and every system in your body depends on water to flush toxins from vital organs, carry nutrients to your cells, and to maintain mental function.

Even mild dehydration will drain your energy, make you tired, and cause fuzzy thinking. Your needs may be higher, depending on temperature and exertion level. Fever, vomiting or diarrhea will also increase your water needs. Generally, you want to be bringing in sufficient fluid for your urine to remain colorless or light yellow.

The Mayo Clinic recommends adults drink 2-3 liters of fluid per day. But that doesn't include the water you will need for other uses, such as cooking, cleaning, hygiene, toilet flushing, laundry, or garden maintenance. So how much total should you be storing? A great rule of thumb is to have two gallons of water per person, per day. This amount should meet all your needs, but it does add up fast. For a family of four, that's 56 gallons for one week.

A good way to approach the problem is to first decide how many days of water you want to maintain, and work the math back from there. Let's say your goal is two weeks of storage. For the family of four, that will require 112 gallons.

Next, think in terms of layers. Bottled water is fine for individual use. They are convenient and easy to carry. But filling your garage with enough bottled water to equal 112 gallons is impractical. So maybe you plan on bottles for only 10% of your total amount.

The next layer would be five-gallon containers. These are heavier and less mobile, but they hold a sizable amount, stack well, and use space more efficiently. They are also small enough to be manageable for tasks like cooking and cleaning. I'd recommend using this level of storage for the next 40% of your total. Using our example total of 112 gallons, you would then want 9 five-gallon containers. Stack them in two piles against a wall, and they won't take up a huge amount of room.

Five gallons of easily storable water security

For the rest of total amount, think big. You want a container that is large, strong, and built to last. Ideally, it also includes a method of collecting new water, because you want more than just water storage, you want water security. That means having a renewable source.

My preferred method is to use a food-grade 55 gallon plastic barrel. It's positioned next to my house's rain gutter, so after a quick trip to Home Depot, I just ran the gutter over to the top of the barrel.

55 gallons of renewable water security

Rainwater now flows from the roof, down the gutter, through a filter screen, and into the barrel. Any overflow goes through a hose back into the rain gutter at ground level. I set the barrel on a base of cinder blocks, so gravity makes it easy to open a hose bib at the bottom, and collect what I need.

While the water is probably ok to drink, I still consider it requiring boiling or treating before consumption. But for many uses, it's fine as-is. And I love knowing I have a renewable system that provides fresh water without electricity. Want more storage? Add more barrels, side by side. http://www.bayteccontainers.com sells them with free shipping.

Water Purification

To make water safe to drink, it should be purified first. If you're in a crisis situation, the last thing you need is to develop stomach problems from contaminated water. Let's look at common methods.

Boiling

Boiling water for one minute will kill the viruses and bacteria that can make you sick. But, it will not do anything to protect you from chemical contaminants, like gasoline, pesticides, lead or other toxins. If your source of water is from the rain, that may not be a concern. But if you're pulling water from a stream that runs through a large farm, the runoff could contain pesticides.

Filtering

We live in a great age for water filtering technology. My current favorite is the Sawyer Mini filter. This small workhorse is a must-have. It's cheap, fits in your pocket, filters down to 0.1 microns, weighs 2 ounces, and can filter 100,000 gallons of water. That is amazing. Even better, it's usable in several ways. Attach it to the included pouch, and you can suck water through it like a straw. Hiking with a hydration bladder? Attach it inline, and drink. I bought four, keep two at home, and put two in our bug out bags.

The Sawyer Mini water filter

Chemical Treatment

The three main ways include iodine, bleach, or chlorine dioxide.

Iodine seems to be going away as a common option, since it adds an offputting taste to the water. If you have kids, you know how hard it can be to get them to drink something they don't like. Why make life hard, when better options are available?

Chlorine dioxide is the active ingredient in many of the tablets you see at camping stores. They work well, and are a great thing to have on hand, especially if you're mobile.

My preferred method for chemical treatment though, is plain old beach. It must be unscented, as the flavorings will make you sick. Just add 8 drops of bleach per gallon of water. Let it sit for 30 minutes, then smell the water. If it smells like a chlorinated pool, you're good to go. If not, repeat the process.

Here's a helpful tip: it's often surprisingly difficult to measure out drops of a liquid, especially from a large, unwieldy container. Make life simple, and pour a little bit of bleach into the cap. Then, take a piece of paper towel and set it into the cap, with some of the paper hanging over the edge. Hold the paper with your finger, and tilt the cap, letting the bleach soak through the paper and drip off the end. Easy!

UV Rays

The suns ultraviolet rays are harmful to microorganisms, and you can use this fact to your advantage. The SODIS (Solar Water Disinfectant) method is used in developing countries as a simple, free method to purify drinking water. Take a clean, transparent, non-colored bottle and fill it with water. A 2-liter soda jug with the wrapper removed works well. The main thing is to use a container that will not block UV rays. Any PET bottle is recommended.

The water must be reasonably clear for this method to work. If you can look down through the bottle and water, and read newspaper print, the water is clear enough. If not, it must be filtered through a bandana first.

Next, lay the bottle out in the sun. If less than half of the sky is clouded over, 6 hours will be enough to completely disinfect the water. If more than half of the sky is covered with clouds, the bottle must be placed in the sun for two consecutive days. That's it. You have disinfected water. While it does take time and sunlight, this method is effective and requires no fuel or chemicals.

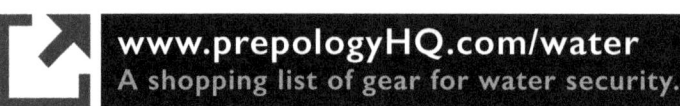
www.prepologyHQ.com/water
A shopping list of gear for water security.

DETOUR → EIGHT DAYS TO TENSION

Looking back at the causes of my interest in prepping, one memory remains clear. Several years ago, we had a big winter ice storm here in the Pacific Northwest. Temperatures plummeted, and strong winds ripped branches from trees over a good piece of Washington. Power was down for over two weeks.

At first, it wasn't bad at all. It was more like an adventure we all shared. The first few days had a great "we're all in this together" camaraderie. A few days later though, things began to shift. By then, the novelty had officially worn off for everyone. All the easy sources of food, water and fuel had been used up.

By the end of the first week, people were braving the roads to look for supplies for themselves and their families. At the time, I was one of those people too. I knew I shouldn't be out driving around on dangerous roads, and possibly adding to the issues faced by work crews, but I had two small, hungry kids at home. The gene that compels us to provide for our family is impossible to ignore.

So there I was, ranging further and further from home, looking for anywhere that might have power. I'd already gotten 12 miles out with no luck. Finally, about 15 miles away, I saw a huge crowd in the parking lot of a Pizza Hut. Somehow, this building had power, and was making pizzas as fast as they could for the horde that packed the place to standing room only. It was a three hour wait for something to eat, but I felt lucky to get it.

As I waited my turn, the edgy feel of the crowd was electric. Nerves were frayed, and patience was short. Whenever someone new arrived, the crowd tensed against them, as if daring them to try to cut in line. Thankfully, there were only glares, grumbles and the occasional yelling match. But as I left, four and a half hours later, I marveled at how volatile the whole scene felt, and it had been only eight days since the storm hit.

Everything returned to normal a few days later, but the experience stayed with me. How would things have gone if the power had been out for longer?

LIGHT

This one is pretty obvious. Having reliable light sources are necessary for comfort and security. Here are some items to have on hand.

Eton/Red Cross Blackout Buddy

These are fantastic lights to start out with, since they're inexpensive, well made, are always ready for use, and have two functions in one device.

Simply plug one into a wall outlet, and you're done. You now have an automatic emergency light that will turn itself on when the power fails. Place a few of these throughout your home, and you'll never stumble around in the dark at 3AM looking for a flashlight.

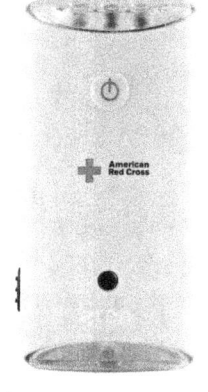

Even better? Each light has a built in battery that charges directly from the wall outlet, so it's always topped off. Grab one of these lights, press a button, and you now have a flashlight, ready to go with you.

At around $11 each, there's no reason not to have 5-6 of these around your house. My only issue with them has been figuring out how to keep my four year old from playing with them. First world problems.

Blackout Buddy

Headlamp

Anyone who's done some camping knows how useful these are. In a nighttime emergency situation, you want your hands free and light on the spot you're looking at. The best way to do that is to have a headlamp. The ones I like have several brightness levels, and are powered by AAA batteries, so I can use rechargeables, and top them off with a solar charger. I'll cover that more soon.

Candles

Candles are a great standby as well, since they store well and don't require batteries. They do introduce a fire risk, but also provide a good psychological boost, as most people find candle light calming.

Liquid paraffin candles are nice to have too. They're sealed units, so they won't spill if tipped over. These typically have burn durations of 100 hours, and optional plastic lenses may be snapped on to improve their brightness.

Flashlight

The recent advances in LED technology have allowed flashlight manufacturers to create some fantastic devices. Companies like Solaray, Streamlight, Surefire, and Fenix all make top-notch lights. Consider getting several small ones that come with belt pouches for easy carry, plus one or two larger models for throwing a ton of light when you really need it.

Do It Yourself! - Homemade Candles

Here's a fun project to do, and it's a very cost effective way to have a large supply of candles on hand. When you're done, you'll have 24 80-hour candles, complete with waterproof containers. Drop some matches in with them, seal the lids, and they'll be ready whenever you need them. They make fun gifts too.

You'll need three items:

» 24 8-ounce Ball Canning Jars

» A pack of 50 candle wicks

» 10-pound bag of soy wax

First, open all the jars and lay them out in the kitchen, near your stove. I left them in the cardboard box they come in, since there's always a little spillage of melted wax.

Next, fill a pot with the wax flakes over medium heat and let it melt fully.

Once the wax is ready, use a ladle or old coffee can to scoop up some wax and pour it carefully into each jar. Fill each one almost to the top.

Next, you're ready to add the wicks. This is the trickiest bit, as they don't want to stand up nicely on their own. I took two rulers, laid them across the tops of one row of jars, then added the wicks between them. Once you have the wicks positioned, slide the rulers together, trapping the exposed wicks in place.

Leave them to cool and harden for a few hours. Once they've firmed up, snip off the excess wick. Voila! Links to buy the items needed are at the URL below.

www.prepologyHQ.com/light
A shopping list of lighting gear.

FOOD

Again, I like to think in terms of layers. Each method of food storage has pros and cons. By layering your food stores, you get the benefits of each.

Just as you planned out how much water your family will need, think about how many calories per person per day you want to plan for. Having enough food for two weeks is a great place to begin.

After you've assembled that, you'll have a good idea of the money/effort/space required. If you then feel you'd like to go further, you'll know how to pretty easily double what you've got.

Meals Ready To Eat (MRE)

In the immediate aftermath of a crisis, there will be a lot to handle. People will be tired, stressed and worried. Keeping meal preparation simple will be a great benefit. While you wouldn't want to live on them for long, MREs are calorie-dense, offer a variety of choices, require no water, and deliver a hot meal without the need for cooking.

I really like the APack brand of MRE. Currently, a case of 12 meals, each containing over 1000 calories, costs $70. Each meal is self-heating, using a simple chemical reaction that heats your meal to 100 degrees in about 12 minutes.

Meals currently include:

» Beef Stew

» Chicken Tetrazzini

» Homestyle Chicken with Noodles & Vegetables

» Pasta with Vegetables in Tomato Sauce

» Southwestern Style Chicken with Black Beans & Rice

» Spaghetti with Meat Sauce.

Each meal comes with a lot of extras too:

» Spork

» Fig bar

» Fuit flavored candies

» Raisins

» Crackers

» Mints

» Seasoning packet

» Pepper

» Towelette

» Meal heater

» Salt water for heater

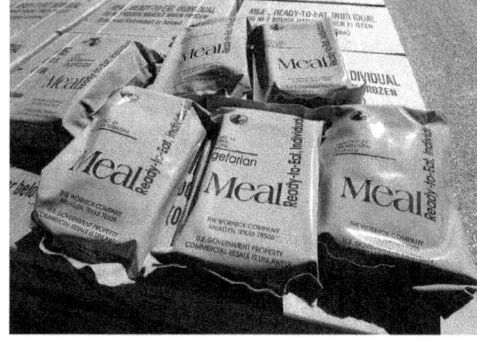

MREs are very convenient to have on hand for ready-made meals.

They also store well. If kept at a temperature of 60 degrees, they'll be good for 48 months.

Overall, that's a lot of value in one box. Think about having a few cases as your first layer of food storage. Check them out at http://readymeal.com

Dehydrated Meals

My second layer of food security is dehydrated meals. These offer great shelf life, more variety than MREs, and are lightweight and compact, which is nice if you have to evacuate. These are routinely used by hikers and campers, so they travel well. The main drawback is that they do require a good source of water for rehydration. They also don't include a heater, so for meals that are better hot, you'll need to heat your water first.

For my money, Mountain House is the gold standard for dehydrated meals. They have a good selection, taste great, and scored the highest in

For long-term storage, dehydrated food are hard to beat.

an independent analysis of shelf life. While they are available in individual pouches, prepologists will be more interested in the buckets of assorted meals.

The Classic Assortment Bucket costs $85, weighs only five pounds, and contains 29 servings of six different meals, including:

» Beef Stroganoff with Noodles

» Chicken Teriyaki with Rice

» Beef Stew

» Lasagna with Meat Sauce

» Noodles & Chicken

» Granola with Milk & Blueberries

These are much smaller serving per pouch, compared to an MRE. Each of the 29 pouch is about 250 calories, so they're meant more as an entree, instead of a complete meal. To rehydrate all 29 pouches requires 21 cups of water.

Mountain House also offers an Essential Assortment Bucket and a Breakfast Assortment Bucket. Additionally, you can get a very wide variety of dehydrated foods in #10 cans too.

Check them out at http://mountainhouse.com

Canned Food

This is a great layer to have in your food security plans, for several reasons.

First, canned foods are likely to include things your family already eats. This is a great advantage in stressful situations.

Second, they store extremely well, even if they are too heavy for easy transport. They also don't require water.

Third, it's easy to gradually build your stockpile of canned food over time. Just make a rule that when you buy any canned food at the store, buy two or three extra for storage. This way, you'll be stocking the exact things your family already likes, without having to spend a lot of money at once.

One key for efficient storage of canned food is have a good system of First In-First Out (FIFO). This just means that as you buy new food, it gets placed behind the older food, so the older supplies get used before the new ones. This automatically keeps your stores fresh, as your normal daily usage will rotate the older stock out.

See http://thrivelife.com for some great systems to keep this simple.

Bulk Food

For your long-term layer, bulk foods are the way to go. Be sure to maintain a good variety of foods. It's easy to think that a large amount of 3-4 basics will be enough, and your family will adapt to a basic menu, but that would be a mistake for long-term situations. People need variety, and good food goes a long way in maintaining morale.

Simple five-gallon buckets are a great option for storing bulk foods. I also like adding a Gamma Seal Lid to my buckets, for easier access. Check out http://www.bayteccontainers.com for good options.

Focus on simple, nutritious foods that store well, such as:

» White rice

» Brown rice (more nutrients, but doesn't store as long)

» Lentils

» Oats

» Beans

» Pasta

» Whole wheat flour

» Trail mix

» Honey

» Barley

» Green peas

» Sugar

» Salt

» Coffee

» Tea

» Hard candy

» Coconut oil

» Dried soup mix

» Powdered milk

» Vinegar

» Hot sauce

» Herbs/Spices

» Baking Soda/Powder

» Alcohol (Vodka/Whiskey)

» Vitamins

How long does it take before people in the largest US city begin rummaging for food in dumpsters? This picture was taken in NYC, four days after hurricane Sandy knocked out power. I begrudge no one taking advantage of an available resource to feed themselves and their family, but this should serve as a wakeup call. With only a little preparation, these people could have avoided such a situation.

Dealing with oxygen

For long-term storage of food, oxygen is the enemy and greatly reduces the shelf life of your stores. If you plan to consistently use your bulk foods, this may not be an issue for you. But if you want your buckets to last for years, you'll need to get as much oxygen out of there as possible. Without oxygen, neither bugs nor bacteria can grow.

One simple method is to fill your bucket with food, then place a paper plate on top. Next, add a piece of dry ice, about five ounces will do.

Leave the cover on, but not tightly secured. As the dry ice sublimates, it will replace the oxygen in the bucket with carbon dioxide. It's heavier than air, so it will settle down, displacing the oxygen out the top. After about five hours, the process should be complete, and you can hammer down the lid. This process works well for seeds, grains, legumes, flour, powdered milk, etc.

Want to take it to the next level, and gain maximum shelf life? Then get some mylar bags and oxygen absorbers. Baytec Containers sells these too. Using this method, you can safely store food up to 25 years or more.

For each bucket, put a 20" x 30" mylar bag in first. Fill the bag with food, and drop an oxygen absorber on top (2000cc for a five-gallon bucket). Heat seal the bag shut, using either a handheld sealer, or an iron. Leave a one inch opening, so you can squeeze out any remaining air, then seal the bag completely.

Living Off The Land

In the event of a serious catastrophe, the idea of escaping to the wilderness and living off the land is strongly appealing. It's an enduring image that many preppers hold dear, and for good reason. We've become increasingly alienated from our food sources. We spend our time becoming more and more specialized in our skills and careers, to the point where for many of us, our chosen profession wouldn't be of much use in a crisis. So the thought of returning to a simpler time and coexisting with nature as our ancestors did, is a siren song that sweetly calls to us, promising a better, more honest way of living.

Unfortunately, like the sirens of Greek mythology, this call would lure most of us to ruin.

It's one thing to go camping for a weekend, or head out for a weeklong hunting trip. Supporting yourself and your family long term in the woods, is something entirely different.

For one thing, people tend to massively underestimate how hard it is to maintain your caloric needs in the wild. Since most of us bring calorically-dense foods with us when we go camping, it's easy to assume alternative, naturally-sourced food sources will suffice. But with the exception of fat (which is rather hard to come by in the woods), the foods you'll likely be finding will be lacking in the energy amounts you'll need to sustain yourself.

This misconception is fueled by TV wilderness experts fixing themselves an easy meal, but failing to point out how little nutrition is actually present. Again, if you're just out for a few days or even weeks, you can easily operate at a calorie deficit. Your body will adjust, and you'll burn stored fat reserves. Then, when you return to civilization, you'll recoup those stores quickly. But if you're out for longer, or having to support multiple people, the picture won't be pretty.

Ross Gilmore did a fantastic breakdown on the numbers involved. You can find the full article on his site at http://woodtrekker.blogspot.com, but here are some basics.

A male under wilderness conditions, performing strenuous activity will need 3,300 calories a day to maintain body weight. To meet that goal, which is for one person only, let's see what kind of hunting would satisfy that goal:

Red Squirrel - With an average of 2.8 ounces of meat each, you'd need to eat 25 squirrels a day. Or 16, if you're careful to also eat the organs and brain.

Rabbit - At 16.8 ounces of meat each, you'd need 4 rabbits per day.

Salmon - Being rich in fat, a six pound salmon would provide about two days worth of food.

Deer - A deer will be a very good food source. With 1,120 ounces of meat, you'll have 18 days of food.

And some plant matter:

Lingonberries - With only 5 calories per ounce, it would take 41 pounds per day

Blueberries - 16 calories per ounce means you'd need to eat 13 pounds per day

Do these numbers seem crazy? As Samuel Thayer, author of the books *Forager's Harvest* and *Nature's Garden*, says, "If this seems like a high volume of food, that's because it is. We have sought, developed, cultivated, and become accustomed to calorie-dense foods for so long that most of us have never been without them. We've never had to eat food in volumes like this. When you realize that a stick of butter has as many calories as two and a half quarts of blueberries or seven pounds of broccoli, you can see why the innate human desire for calorie-rich, low-fiber food developed."

Now obviously, you'd be mixing and matching various food sources, but you can still gain some perspective on the job required. Many experienced hunters go out and return empty-handed. And people who have learned the myriad skills involved in hunting game typically take several times more than beginners can manage.

As if that's not enough reality for you, consider that there simply won't be enough large animals to go around. You have to assume that if things have gotten bad enough for you to bug out to the hills, then a lot of other people are having the same idea too. Animals are pretty good at staying alive. When humans encroach on an area, game tends to leave. With dozens, if not hundreds, of loud, smelly, inexperienced humans start roaming the area, it won't be long before it becomes what's known as an "empty forest", or one that has lost any mammals, birds or reptiles that weight over a few pounds.

To put a number on it, how many humans do you think can sustainably take game from a piece of land? Tropical ecologist Rhett Harrison puts the number at *one human per square kilometer.*

Food for thought.

MEDICAL KIT

This is one area that gets a lot of attention from preppers, and the marketplace has taken notice. Prebuilt medical kits are everywhere, promising to give you everything you need in one easy package. While I'm sure there are some good kits out there, my advice is to build your own instead. Generally, those kits are working hard to hit a price point, so the quality of the various items is not what you want to rely on when someone needs medical attention. Plus, it's better to assemble your own kit because only you know your needs. A single guy needs a very different kit that a family of four, with a toddler.

The process can seem daunting, I will admit. There's a lot of things to consider, and it's tempting to just buy a premade kit and call it done.

 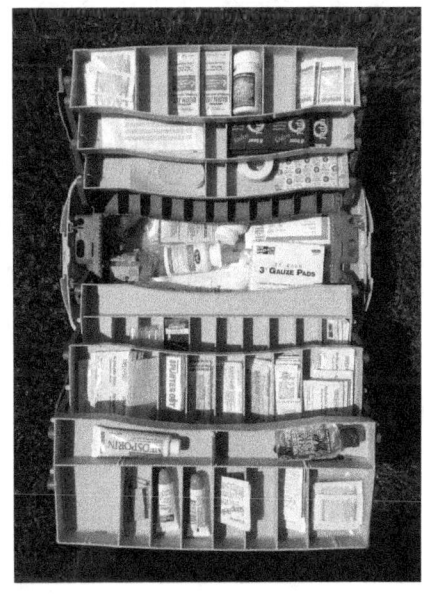

What I did was to start with a good case to store everything, then thought about the types of injuries that could occur. After that, I compiled lists from other people who had already assembled their kit. I borrowed some ideas, substituted others, and just did as much research as I could into each item, so I found the best quality option.

While you could buy a dedicated medical case, I found you could get almost exactly the same thing for far less by getting a fisherman's tackle box instead. Voila! Instant $80 savings.

To give you a roadmap to follow, I've put together a checklist for you at:

www.prepologyHQ.com/medical
A shopping list of items for your medical kit.

Just follow the links listed there for my exact brand recommendations. It covers everything from stomach upset to first-aid to wound treatment. The nice thing about putting the kit together is that you don't have to do it all at once. Start with a case, and some of the basics. Then, slowly add to it over time, checking things off the list.

Books

Having some good medical resource materials as part of your preps is a necessity. Unless you have a doctor in the family, make sure to include a few books on emergency medicine, just in case.

Some recommendations:

The Survival Medicine Handbook, by Joseph Alton

Wilderness Medicine, by William Forgey

Where There Is No Doctor, by David Werner

Where There Is no Dentist, by Murray Dickson

POWER

We've become so accustomed to electricity, it can be disconcerting when it suddenly isn't there. Sure, having no power was completely normal for people 130 years ago, but they didn't have the benefit of refrigerators and iPhones. These days, such things may not be absolute necessities, but they sure do make life easier.

In terms of alternate means of electricity, the recent announcements about the Tesla battery pack and solar panel combo sounds amazing, but still a ways off for most of us.

Generator

The next best option would be owning a generator and using gasoline to keep the lights on. They do offer a lot of power, but also come with some serious drawbacks. They're not cheap, they require a constant supply of fuel, they produce carbon monoxide, and they're noisy. They also tend to highlight your home as one that has resources. The sound of a running generator carries pretty far when everyone around you is out of power.

But if the tradeoffs are worth it to you, the first step is to calculate how much wattage you'll be using. This determines how large of a generator you'll need. Honda has a handy wattage calculator at http://powerequipment.honda.com/generators/wattage-calculator. Just plug in what appliances you want to be able to keep running, and it will calculate the wattage load required, and offer suggestions for models that can accommodate.

Inverter

A much cheaper backup option might be an inverter, which is a device that converts DC power to AC. For less than $100, you could have a model that connects to your car battery and provides two AC outlets. By running the car for a few hours a day, it would be enough to keep food from spoiling in the freezer, or to charge up a laptop.

Solar

Recent developments in solar panels for hiking and camping have really made these attractive. Companies like Sunjack and Goal Zero offer some great products in the 7 to 20 watt range. These folding, portable panels are designed to be carried by hikers, so they store away well when not needed. They certainly won't run appliances, but for keeping your phone, laptop, or rechargeable batteries topped off, they're hard to beat.

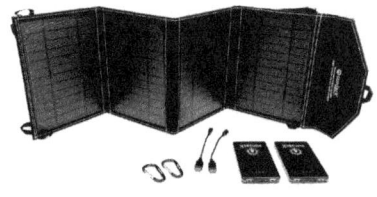

Hand-Crank

Emergency radios like the Eton Red Cross model shown here are great additions to your kit for many reasons, but the hand crank also allows you to manually recharge USB devices like a cell phone. To get a decent charge does take work, but it's doable. Since these devices are such great multi-taskers, it's really useful to have one around.

 **www.prepologyHQ.com/power**
A shopping list of items for generating power.

COOKING

While MREs are great for a while, you need a proper cooking method for your food. If nothing else, having the ability to boil water is important for safe drinking water, sanitation, and comfort items like coffee.

For most people, the first thought is the backyard grill. And why not? You probably have some spare propane, and grilled food is delicious. Depending on the length of your emergency situation, that may suffice.

But if you want to be prepared beyond that, it's tough to beat the ubiquity of wood as a cooking source. Building an open fire is always an option, but while it's a favorite morale booster, it's not terribly efficient. If you rely on open fire cooking for all your meals, you'll find yourself hauling way more firewood than you want, and having to range further and further to collect it.

To make the most of your wood supply, take a look at some of the biomass stoves available. Keep in mind these are for outdoor use only! Some great examples:

EcoZoom Rocket Stove

With thick, insulated walls, the Ecozoom is a high efficiency cooker. You feed wood (or charcoal) in at the bottom, and place a cooking pan on top. Like all biomass burners, this is a great way to get the most from your wood supply.

It also doesn't require large chunks of fuel. Just keep feeding in sticks as needed.

SilverFire Scout

This outdoor stove is specially designed to facilitate secondary combustion, or to ignite the gasses and smoke that would normally escape. The result is a cleaner, more efficient fire that uses less fuel to do the same work. The trick is in the outer baffle that prewarms air as it rises up the sides, then is funneled into the upper combustion area. Watch a video of it in action on Youtube, and you'll see the ring of secondary flame near the top. It's quite beautiful, too.

Bushbox XL

The most portable of the options, this German-made, stainless steel outdoor stove folds flat for easy storage or transport in a bugout bag. Feed it twigs/branches/leaves, and it can boil half a liter of water in three minutes. Alternatively, use charcoal, wood pellets, dry dung, or Esbit fuel tabs. Twin trivets support any size pot, or use the flat plate for grilling meat.

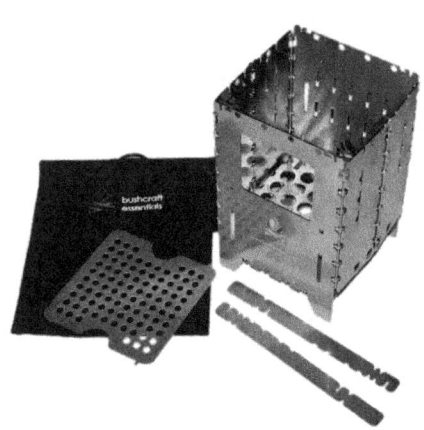

www.prepologyHQ.com/cooking
A shopping list of items for cooking/boiling water.

FIREARMS

The issue of gun ownership can be a contentious one, and I don't want to delve into the politics. A premise of this book is to use fact-based decisions, so let's start with a few data points.

One of President Obama's executive actions was to commission a $10 million study into gun use, investigated by the CDC. They came back with some interesting findings:

» In 2010, incidents in the U.S. involving firearms injured or killed more than 105,000 Americans, of which there were twice as many nonfatal firearm-related injuries (73,505) than deaths.

» Between the years 2000 and 2010, firearm-related suicides significantly outnumbered homicides for all age groups, annually accounting for 61 percent of the more than 335,600 people who died from firearm-related violence in the United States.

» Whether gun restrictions reduce firearm-related violence is an unresolved issue.

» There is no evidence that passage of right-to-carry laws decrease or increase violence crime.

» Violent crimes, including homicides specifically, have declined in the past five years.

» Self-defense can be an important crime deterrent.

Are there risks in keeping a firearm in the house? Yes, of course. But there are also risks associated with storing dangerous chemicals for cleaning, driving a car, and mowing your yard. According to the CDC, "Americans in general are more likely to die of motor vehicle traffic accidents, accidental poisoning, accidental falls, accidental suffocation, accidental drowning, or other unclassified accidents than they are to die of an accidental shooting."

So, what's the bottom line? I do recommend including one or more firearms in your preparations. Shooting is an important skill both for self-defense and hunting. Plus, it's fun! Obviously, you want to be familiar with federal, state and local laws related to owning/storing/transporting a firearm. And just as obviously, you need to learn to handle it safely and effectively.

The question of which guns to buy is a very subjective one. I'll recommend a few below, but my best advice is to join a local firing range. Start with their beginner class, to make sure you know the basics. Then, spend an afternoon trying a bunch out. Most ranges are happy to rent you a gun at a time. Buy some ammo, and bring a notepad for taking notes about each one right after you fire it.

It can get overwhelming trying to remember the pros and cons of each gun, especially after you've gone through a half-dozen.

After each firing, try to decide if the most recent gun was better or worse than whichever one is your current favorite. That way, you always have a current frontrunner to compare against.

Handguns

Small, light, and convenient. It's tough to beat the utility a handgun offers. While they don't have the range than a long gun does, they're also easy to carry in a holster, leaving your hands free. Which means you're more likely to carry it. Like the old saying, "the best camera is the one you have with you", your gun can't help you if you left it behind. They are also concealable, which is good for not attracting attention.

Glock 17

Handguns break down into two main categories: revolvers and semiautomatics. People who choose revolvers tend to be more concerned with reliability. Since the mechanism of a revolver is simpler, the idea is that it's less prone to jamming. However, while semi-autos do add some complexity, they also carry a lot more bullets. So, like most things in life: TANSTAAFL (There Ain't No Such Thing As A Free Lunch).

Glock is an excellent choice for an all-around pistol. They're remarkably durable, reliable, and easy to handle. Their performance in inclement weather and conditions is legendary. Just the type of attributes you want in a crisis. I'm also a fan of Sig Sauer's handguns.

Shotguns

A shotgun is a great utility weapon, since it can be loaded with differing ammunition, depending on the role it should play. They can send a cloud of

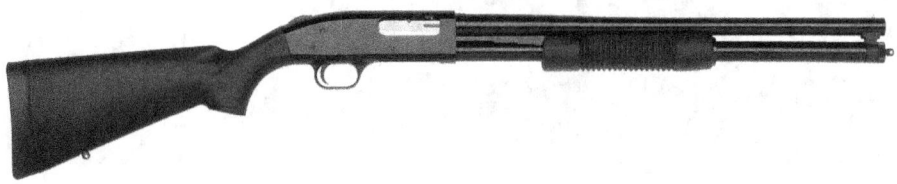

Mossberg 500

small projectiles at small game, like rabbits or birds or be loaded with a solid slug for larger game such as deer. With the addition of various chokes, you can set how much scatter you desire. There are even less-than-lethal shells available.

The classic 12 gauge is always a fine choice, but for those nervous about recoil, check out the Mossberg .410 models.

.22 Rifles

Possibly the prepper's best first gun purchase. .22 ammunition is cheap, and perfect for target practice and hunting small game. It's an easy rifle to fire, so if you have a spouse who's less than excited about shooting, a .22 is a gentle first experience. My favorite is the Ruger 10/22 takedown rifle, which breaks down in two pieces for easy transport, and even comes with its own case.

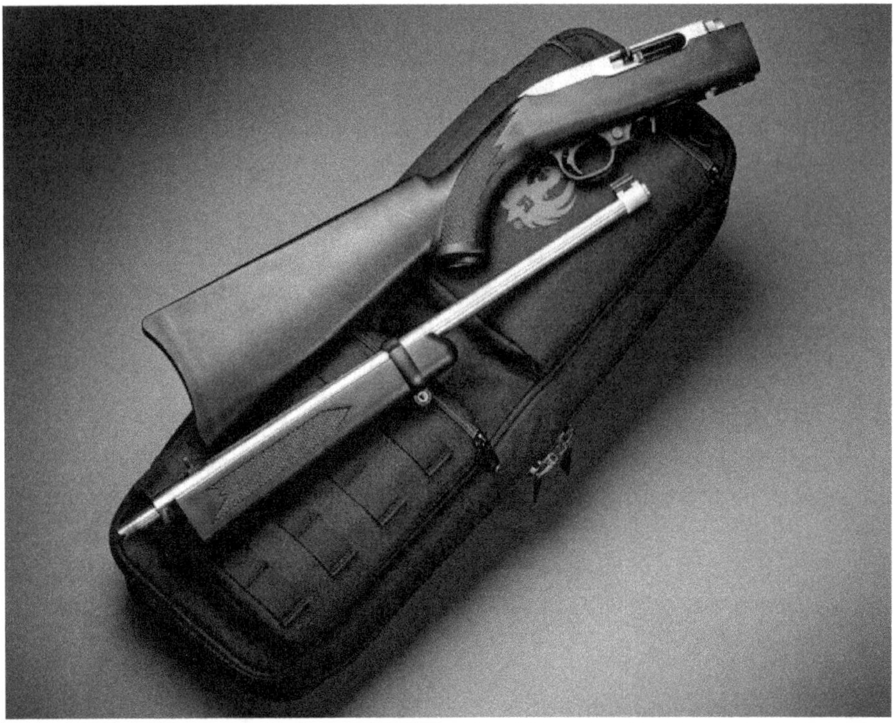

Ruger .22 Takedown

High Power Rifles

For the maximum in range and accuracy, nothing beats the long arms. Experienced shooters are accurate out to 1000 yards, and with some practice, most anyone can take game at 400 yards. Long range shooting has always been a favorite of mine. To place a round far downrange on target requires a unique set of skills, but I find them enjoyable to work on.

My choice in this category? The Winchester Model 70. A few years back, it celebrated its 75th anniversary. For a rifle to have that kind of longevity says

Winchester Model 70

a lot. The MOA trigger system is excellent, and the free floating barrel means maximum accuracy. This rifle comes in a wide variety of versions, but take a look at the Extreme Weather SS for top-of-the-line weather durability.

Bottom Line

Ideally, I would recommend owning one firearm from each of these categories. They do represent an investment, but you would be well equipped for any type of protection or game hunting scenario.

DETOUR → THE WAFFLE HOUSE INDEX

There are several official ways to gauge how much damage a storm has done to an area, but none are as colorful as the Waffle House Index.

The term was coined by FEMA administration Craig Fugate in 2011. In case you don't know, Waffle House has quite the deserved reputation for staying open during extreme weather, and for reopening quickly, albeit with a special, limited menu.

According to Fugate, "If you get there and the Waffle House is closed? That's really bad. That's where you go to work."

The Index has three levels, based on the extent of operations and service at the restaurant following a storm:

Green: the restaurant is serving a full menu, indicating the restaurant has power and damage is limited.

Yellow: the restaurant is serving a limited menu, indicating there may be no power or only power from a generator or food supplies may be low.

Red: the restaurant is closed, indicating severe damage.

Because the restaurants have a disaster plan and a cut-down menu prepared for times when there is no power or limited supplies, the Waffle House Index rarely reaches the red level.

COMMUNICATIONS

In most crisis situations, it's a safe bet that regular communications will be down, at least temporarily. The cell phones we all have in our pocket depend on powered cell towers. Normal phones rely on transmission lines. Email and instant messaging go dark without the internet infrastructure in place.

Having another option for communications means you'll be safer, know more, and have more options. Consider just a few of the things possible with reliable comms:

» Checking in on family/relatives

» Staying in touch with team members foraging for food or supplies

» Communicating with others in a convoy

» Coordinating with others for security or rescue operations

There are many choices for backup communication gear. Let's look at the main categories and the pros/cons of each of them.

Solar/Hand Crank Radios

While these are receive-only radios, they absolutely deserve a place in your gear. The best ones can run on batteries, but also have a solar panel and a hand crank for recharging. They'll let you listen in to the AM/FM stations, as well as the NOAA weather channels. They usually include an LED flashlight and a USB port for powering your cellphone. That's a lot of bang for the buck.

FRS Radios

These are the normal walkie-talkies you see at Walmart. FRS (Family Radio Service) units are very popular for staying in touch between two cars driving together, camping trips, or on the ski slopes. They use a non-removable antenna, so you can't hook one up to a car roof antenna for better range. While they advertise ranges of 18-30 miles, that assumes a direct line of sight, which is hardly ever realistic. 1-3 miles is more typical. However, they are user friendly and affordable.

If privacy is critical, these may not be your best bet, although newer models allow you to set a privacy code for the channel you're on. So someone would need to be within range of you, and on the same channel and privacy code before they'd hear your conversation.

There are no secrets to success.
It is the result of preparation, hard work,
and learning from failure.
Colin Powell

MURS Radios

While less well-known, MURS radios offer a nice step up in functionality. They permit four times more output power than FRS units. Their frequencies bend over hills better, but FRS signals do bounce off surfaces better. You may connect a MURS radio to an external antenna, like a car roof system, and expect three to ten times the range of FRS radios.

CB Radios

Made famous by truckers, Citizen's Band radio is a high-frequency, no license required system. Depending on terrain, their range is 5-20 miles. They have 40 channels, and are limited to an output of 4 watts. Each channel is a different frequency, with channel 9 being used for emergencies.

Ham Radio

This is a big subject, and could easily fill another book. Haw radios offer the best level of performance, but as always, there is no free lunch. They require training and an FCC license to operate. Proficiency in morse code is no longer a requirement. The lowest certification is Technician Class, providing access to UHF and VHF bands, plus the 6 meter and 10 meter bands.

Ham operators are frequently utilized in search and rescue communications, and often keep communications alive when all other options in a crisis have failed. Many hams are prepared to stay on the air during emergencies with backup power. They may transmit at much higher power levels, and access any frequency their license allows, rather than choosing from a small list of channels. The community is welcoming of newcomers, and experienced hams ("Elmers"), are often eager to mentor new ham operators.

DETOUR → JUST IN TIME INVENTORY

For any serious emergency, we need to remember how fragile our supply lines are. Just In Time inventory techniques and global trade have done amazing things for our standard of living. But those same systems, designed for efficiency and low cost, are not well adapted to the realities of a crisis.

The wise person plans ahead. When the storm waters rise, it's too late to hit the stores for food, water or fuel. By then, you're just part of the problem. You're pulling scarce resources out of the available supply just when they're needed most. By thinking and acting beforehand, and slowly pulling what resources you need from the system at times of plenty, you impact no one.

Preparedness brings peace of mind. The point is to enjoy life, not let paranoia run rampant. I prefer a mindful, measured approach to risk-assessment. A fearful attitude about the future sucks the joy from the present.

SANITATION

Keeping yourself and your environment clean is critically important in an emergency situation. People will be already be tired and stressed, two factors that will impact productivity. Don't let illness or infections contribute and make a bad situation worse than it needs to be.

Food Prep

Be meticulous about surface areas and tools you use for preparing food, especially if you're handling fish, game or poultry. Cross-contamination happens easily if you're not paying attention. If practical, use the same knives/tools/cutting surface every time, and develop a routine of cleaning them after each cooking session with a diluted bleach solution of one tablespoon per gallon of water. To be effective, the solution must stay on the surface for at least one minute. At this concentration, it's fine to let things air dry, in the sun if possible. If you have a spray bottle, that makes an easy way to cover surfaces, while also not wasting your solution.

Dishware

Washing dishes is pretty simple, if you follow a consistent plan. The four bucket method is a standard way to clean dishes in the field, and it will work great during a crisis too:

Bucket 1: Cold water for scrubbing off bits of food

Bucket 2: Hot, soapy water for scrubbing plates and bowls

Bucket 3: Hot water for rinsing the soap off

Bucket 4: Cold water with a capful of bleach gives a final, sanitizing rinse

First Aid

Be aggressive about dealing with cuts and abrasions. A little attention early can prevent a more serious problem later. Keep some Neosporin or povidone iodine handy. I made up a first-aid mini kit for the kitchen. It's just an Altoids tin with the basic things to treat common kitchen injuries: bandaids, burn gel, a small vial of povidone iodine, and some pain killers. If someone slices their finger open, it's nice to have what you need right there.

Toilets

If your water supply is cut off, you can still flush toilets with a bucket of water, assuming you have an alternate supply, such as rainwater. When needed, just quickly dump a bucket of water into the toilet bowl, and let physics take it from there. One or two quarts should be sufficient.

For the more rugged style of waste management (solids only), a five-gallon bucket is a classic standby. First, line the bucket with a garbage bag, preferably the heavier contractor's grade. Feel free to mount a toilet seat on top for comfort. If toilet paper becomes in short supply, keep a stash of baby wipes nearby. And don't forget to have hand sanitizer too. For odor control, toss in some cat litter, sawdust, dirt or ash from your wood fire.

Bathing

For maximum comfort, a solar camp shower will be much appreciated. Just fill it with water, hang in the sun, and enjoy. Camping stores like REI have a nice selection of these.

Next down on the comfort scale would be a thermos of hot water and a washcloth or bandana. You'd be surprised how much better you feel after a good face scrub with hot water though.

While a quick wipedown with baby wipes may not be ideal, it's been good enough for a lot of our troops in the field.

Teeth

Don't forget to keep your teeth brushed. In a crisis, it may not be your first priority, but when possible, it will keep you healthier and help add a sense of normalcy.

Laundry

Assuming your electric washing machine is not an option, a simple alternative is a five-gallon bucket filled with four gallons of hot water. Add a tablespoon of liquid soap, then apply a plunger for 5-10 minutes of vigorous swirling action. One load should handle one person's clothing at a time. After the wash, wring them out and hang in the sun to dry.

⟦DETOUR →⟧ THIS WAR OF MINE

It's great to study and read about prepping, but sometimes you can learn a lot from a whole new medium. This War Of Mine is an award winning video game that puts you in role of the civilians caught in a war zone.

You'll get to know each person in your group, and learn their history along the way. Each person has different strengths and weaknesses too. While Bruno can carry a lot back from scavenging missions, he's also slow. More interested in improving your home situation? Then you'll want Marin on your team, since he can build house upgrades like a cook stove or moonshine still with fewer resources.

It's worth checking out, as it puts you in the middle of a myriad number of survival decisions. As one member of your group goes out scavenging for the night, do you let the others sleep, and risk getting hit by burglars because no one was on guard? How do you distribute the limited food, bandages and medicine you may have? Do you help your neighbors, or steal from them?

The answers to questions like these are not as clear, once you're in a survival situation. While no game can fully prepare you for such a situation, I can say that after playing this for a week, I began having dreams about the people in my group. http://11bitstudios.com

FUEL

We've all seen the pictures of people standing in long lines at the gas station, red fuel cans in hand, waiting for hours to get a few gallons. Don't be one of those people.

With just a little forethought, it's actually pretty easy to safely store fuel in case of emergency. Having a few extra propane tanks around is a fairly obvious good idea, and is trivial, since it stores so easily. But what about gasoline? Maybe you have a generator, and want to ensure a fuel supply for it to keep your refrigerator and lights going. Or perhaps you need to

evacuate to another location, and don't want to get caught with an empty tank.

Whatever the goal, it's so much easier to buy the fuel now, and store it properly. Leave the gas lines to those who couldn't be bothered to plan ahead.

You can find good fuel cans most anywhere, from Amazon to Home Depot. I recommend five-gallon cans, either metal or the ubiquitous plastic. Keep in mind the standard color scheme when you buy them:

Red = Gasoline

Blue = Kerosene

Yellow = Diesel

Follow this convention for safety. You don't want to be pouring gasoline into your kerosene heater.

I'm a fan of the metal jerry can style myself. They're especially durable, and they're a standard size and shape to be secured to a vehicle. You can find many aftermarket accessories designed for mounting jerry cans to your bug out vehicle.

Safety

Check your local fire codes, but generally homeowners are limited to storing 25 gallons of gasoline, in approved containers of five gallons or less each. Be sure your homeowner's policy allows what you have, as well. In case of a fire, you don't want to provide them an easy reason to refuse your claim.

Gasoline is obviously flammable, so store it well away from heat sources, such as the sun, a hot water heater, space heater, or a furnace. Keep 50 feet from any ignition sources, like a pilot light. Remember that gasoline vapors are heavier than air, and can travel along the floor to ignition sources. Never smoke where your fuel is stored.

Never mix gasoline with kerosene or diesel. Don't use gasoline in kerosene heaters.

Shelf Life

What most people don't know is that gasoline and diesel fuel will not store for long. According to BP:

"As diesel gets older a fine sediment and gum forms in the diesel brought about by the reaction of diesel components with oxygen from the air. The fine sediment and gum will block fuel filters, leading to fuel starvation and the engine stopping. Frequent filter changes are then required to keep the engine going. The gums and sediments do not burn in the engine very well and can lead to carbon and soot deposits on injectors and other combustion surfaces."

This process happens within 2-3 months. Oxidized gasoline will appear darker, and may smell sour. It's a little tricky to know how long untreated gas will remain good, since you don't know how old it is when you pump it. Your gasoline could be fresh from the refinery, or already be a month old.

The good news is there's a solution. By adding a small amount of fuel stabilizer to your gas storage, you can increase it's shelf life to a year or more. Some people claim to be getting good use of stabilized fuel after three years, but since I need to rotate it out anyway, I just plan on one year. The one I use is called Pri-G. One bottle will treat 256 gallons of gasoline, so it's a great deal. Just add a little to your empty gas can, then pump in the gas. The two will mix thoroughly. Try not to leave a lot of air space at the top, then seal the can firmly. Good to go for a year!

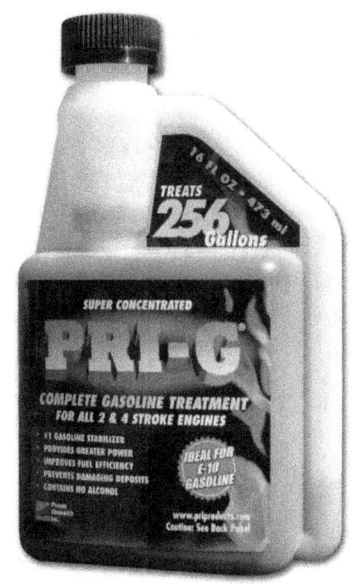

Don't forget to label your fuel cans with the date they should be used by. Rotating your supply is a best practice. As your fuel reaches it's "use-by" date, just add it to your car, and replace it with a fresh batch of gas/stabilizer.

HEATING

If you live in a cold climate, keeping your home heated during a crisis could be a life or death situation. But don't let the need for warmth drive you to do stupid things.

Carbon monoxide is a silent, odorless killer. Every year, trying to stay warm, people die from things like burning their charcoal grill indoors, or running a fuel heater without ventilation. According to the Florida Department of Health, "every year more than 500 Americans die from accidental exposure to carbon monoxide". CO is created by combustion of carbon-containing materials, and it forms when there is not enough oxygen to produce carbon dioxide, such as when operating a stove or an internal combustion engine in an enclosed space. Get a carbon monoxide detector for your house!

Carbon Monoxide detector/alarm

Electric space heaters don't have this problem, but if you're prepping for a winter crisis, you probably won't have power. Instead, think about propane. While it doesn't match the energy density of kerosene, it's safer, cheap, and stores very well. It also doesn't have the unpleasant smell associated with kerosene heaters.

A great propane heater is the Buddy series of heaters from Mr. Heater. The Portable Buddy has a single ceramic heating plate, uses a 1 lb. cylinder for fuel, and can heat 200 square feet. Its larger brother, the Big Buddy, has two plates, two 1 lb. cylinders, and heats 400 square feet. With an optional hose, both models can be connected to a standard 20 lb. propane tank. However, the tank must remain outdoors, so plan to feed the hose through a window for safe operation. This is a good idea anyway, since you'll want to crack a window for ventilation.

Here are some other ideas to consider:

Mr. Heater propane heater

Mind the drafts

If you're hunkering down for an extended time, place draft blockers along the bottom of all your doors. Most anything will work, like towels, sheets, even unused clothing. This will help section off your house into smaller units, and keep your heating efforts contained to where you want them.

Insulate the windows

Sealing the air space just in front of your windows can help tremendously in reducing heat loss. While some people talk about using bubblewrap for this purpose, that seems impractical to me. For one, you'll lose the ability to see outside. And second, who is going to have huge rolls of the stuff on hand? A better solution are 3M's window insulation kits. These are readymade, transparent films that help keep your home's heat inside. Each kit is good for five windows, and they store easily away.

Focus on one room

Rather than heating the whole house, choose one room to focus on. Most modern homes have an open floor plan that combines the living room with the kitchen. This may be a good choice. Use blankets or plastic sheeting to section that area off from the rest of the house, and you'll make the job of keeping it warm much easier.

Kotatsu

In Japan, few houses are built with central heating, and most are not well insulated. So a common feature is the kotatsu, which is a large table with a heater underneath and a thick blanket draped over the whole thing. Families can sit around the table with their legs under the blanket, enjoying the toasty warmth. Typical versions have an electric heater mounted to the underside of the table. In the event of a cold weather crisis, something like this could be just the thing to raise spirits. Not only does everyone get to warm up, the design brings everyone together for conversation, meals or games. For safety, you obviously need to be careful about what heat source you use.

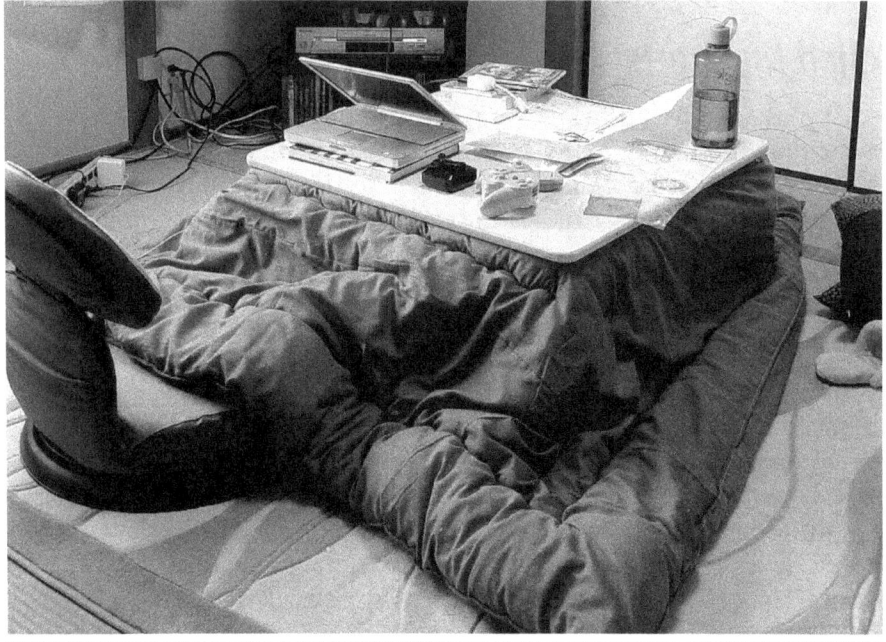

A typical modern Japanese Kotatsu

Get Outside

Rather than staying indoors and fretting about how cold the house is, force everyone to get out a bit, weather permitting. Even if cold outside, the sunshine will improve morale, and coming back inside will feel comforting.

Indoor camping

Pitch a tent in the living room! My kids love this one, even at normal times. Toss in a blanket, a few pillows and a book. You'll have fun, and feel warmer inside.

Dress in layers

Heat the body, not the room. For maximum warmth, start with a base layer of silk or synthetic thermal underware. Next, add a comfortable layer. Cotton is not recommended in rainy conditions, since wet cotton will suck away your body heat. Then add a warmth layer of wool or synthetic. Even when wet, these materials still preserve your body heat. Don't forget a warm hat. If going outside, a windbreaker will be helpful too.

Solar Soda Can Heater

Google this for a lot of examples of how people have made their own solar heater. The basic idea is to build an enclosed box around stacks of empty soda cans that have had holes punched in the bottoms. Cool air comes in the bottom of the box, flows through the cans, picking up heat along the way, then comes out the top, ready to be funneled into your home. Some designs are... less than ideal. But many work great, offering a temperature differential of over 100 degrees.

DO YOU FEEL LUCKY, PUNK?

Prepologists deal with facts, not unfounded fears. So here are the odds of dying from various causes. Perspective is a good thing.

Heart disease: 1 in 6

Cancer: 1 in 7

Stroke: 1 in 28

Hospital infections: 1 in 38

Car accident: 1 in 112

Drowning: 1 in 1043

Fire: 1 in 1418

Cataclysmic Storm: 1 in 46,044

Lightning: 1 in 136,011

Earthquake: 1 in 148,756

Flood: 1 in 175,803

ENTERTAINMENT

It's strange, but I've heard from quite a few preppers who diligently stockpile food, water, ammo, medical supplies and fuel, but scoff at the idea of entertainment needs. I suppose they don't care about something so frivolous because they'll be too busy fending off the hordes or rooting through deadwood for grubs.

At first glance, I get it. When we picture a survival situation, we tend to paint a dire scene, devoid of laughter or happiness. Of course, if that's the future you see for yourself, then you must not think much of your preps. After all, isn't the whole point to be prepared? If it's all doom and gloom for you and yours, then why aren't you taking steps to avoid that situation?

It may help if we use a different word. How about "morale"? Now, that's a whole other story. Morale is vital to troop efficiency. Morale matters to the military, so it must be ok to focus on. *Molon labe!*

But remember, you're not leading the Spartans at Thermopylae, or a fire team in Afghanistan. You're responsible for the well being of your family. To them, morale means feeling safe and comfortable, both physically and mentally. Keeping them in good spirits matters as much as keeping them well-fed, because a good attitude can get them through when times get tough.

The specifics of what will accomplish this goal will depend on the age and temperament of those around you, of course, but some things to consider having around include:

» Books, for each person's interest

» Portable DVD player

» Board games

» Playing cards

» Musical instruments

» Kid's toys

» Drawing supplies

» Stuffed animals

» Football

» Dominos

» Yahtzee

» Jump rope

» Chess board

» Crosswords/Suduku

Keeping everyone occupied will make everyone happier.

Yes, depending on the specifics of your situation, there may be little time for entertainment.

But for the majority of the events you're likely to face, there will be long stretches of downtime, and even boredom. Being prepared for this situation is a fairly easy task.

THE GOLDEN HORDE

Originally, the Golden Horde referred to the Mongol Armies of the 13th century. Known for vicious raids, they eventually controlled over 2.3 million square miles.

Many preppers believe that in times of emergency, the population in densely-packed cities will flee, spreading out into the surrounding areas. Seeking resources, this 'horde' will be desperate, hungry and dangerous. Does history support this concept? Well, yes and no. It depends on the disaster.

Consider something like the recent Argentinian financial collapse. The depression caused widespread unemployment, riots, the fall of a government, a default on the country's foreign debt, the rise of alternative currencies and the end of the peso's fixed exchange rate to the US dollar. From 1998 to 2002, the economy shrank by 28%. Seven out of ten Argentine children were poor in 2002. By all accounts, this is a full blown emergency situation.

So, did the horde spew from the cities, to ransack the surrounding areas? No, not really. Argentina did not see a huge exodus of people fleeing the cities. If anything, the opposite was true. People left the country and came to the cities seeking work.

Bear in mind that with decent governance, even a crash like Argentina's can be turned around relatively quickly. By 2005, Argentina's GDP exceeded pre-crisis levels. A year later, Argentina repaid its IMF loans in full. By 2010, only 7% of bonds were unpaid to investors. So for those on the ground, eight years is a hell of a long time to suffer. But from a global economic perspective, that's pretty damn impressive.

Now consider a localized natural disaster like Hurricane Katrina. In that case, there was massive evacuation of the population. FEMA instituted Contraflow, allowing both sides of highways to run out of the city. And did it ever work. In a two-day stretch, 500,000 vehicles carried over 1 million people out of New Orleans. Yes, many of them had a destination in mind, like distant relatives who agreed to take them in. But still, that's a huge amount of resource pressure on the surrounding area.

So while this phenomenon is real in some cases, it just depends on the type of danger people face.

PRECIOUS METALS

Another sacred cow of prepping is the idea of storing wealth in precious metals like silver or gold. The thinking is that in times of massive financial collapse, these metals will serve as a stable currency when other traditional options (like US dollars) will not.

While I don't worry about this here in the US, I do recognize that those in other countries may see things differently. If you might find yourself forced to cross a border with only whatever you can carry, then sewing some gold coins into your clothing makes good sense.

In sum, the fear is massive inflation leading to a loss of purchasing power. Since governments can simply print more currency whenever they wish, there's a fear of hyperinflation, or that currency someday having far less buying power than it currently does. Generally, a rate of 50% or more is labelled hyperinflation. At that rate, a junior cheeseburger deluxe at Wendy's, which costs about one dollar today, would cost $130 a year from now.

Could that happen here in the US? Anything's possible, but I wouldn't bank on it. So to speak. :)

Hyperinflation is a product of large government deficits financed primarily by money creation (printing new currency) instead of taxation or borrowing. As such, the phenomenon is often associated with wars, their aftermaths, political upheavals, or other events that make it difficult for the country to tax the population.

But things get ugly fast when you combine two forces: a sharp decrease of tax revenue with a strong desire to maintain the status quo. In that a case, a nation can only borrow its way out of trouble. But if other countries consider the situation too risky to get involved, then you will have a serious hyperinflation event.

Curiously, the US has already experienced such a crisis. During the Revolutionary War, when the Continental Congress authorized the printing of paper currency called continental currency, the monthly inflation rate reached a peak of 47% in November 1779. These notes depreciated rapidly, giving rise to the expression "not worth a continental." One cause of the inflation was counterfeiting by the British, who ran a press on the HMS Phoenix, moored in New York Harbor. The counterfeits were advertised and sold almost for the price of the paper they were printed on.

But that was a long time ago, and things have changed since then. Currently, the Gross Domestic Product of the US economy is $16,768,100 million, which is by far the largest of any country on the planet. China comes in second, at roughly half of that. Japan is next, at half of China's GDP. It's easy to find stories of rampant devaluation. The 1998-2002 financial crisis in Argentina comes to mind. The Economist puts it this way: "Yes, America occasionally budgets recklessly. But it has a very deep, very broad, and very strong civil society, buttressed by levels upon levels of private and public, formal and informal institutions. These institutions, and many like them across rich economies, are generally very good at preventing governments from doing disastrous things."

Monetary policy run amok. In 2009, this note wouldn't even buy a bus ticket.

Of course, none of this stops the Chicken Littles from spreading gloom, and who often have a vested interest in spreading fear.

Newsmax.com darling Robert Wiedemer, author of the New York Times best-selling book Aftershock, stated in an interview, "The data is clear, 50% unemployment, a 90% stock market drop, and 100% annual inflation... starting in 2012."

None of these things came close to being true.

The US unemployment rate was 8% in Jan, 2012 and has fallen steadily ever since.

The stock market? The S&P 500, an index of the largest 500 corporations in the country, was at 1300 at the start of 2012, and has risen ever since to today's value of 2100.

How about inflation? We were at 1.7% in 2012. Today? 0%.

It's hard to imagine a pundit being more wrong. But fear sells books, and humans are hard-wired to respond to it. We should all try to do better.

Bottom line

If it comforts you to put some cash into gold, feel free. But understand that you may get a lot more utility by putting that cash into things you know that you'll need in an emergency, like food, water, or... cash.

YOUR COMMUNITY

This is a tricky one.

On one hand, you may want to engage with your neighbors, and get them up to speed with being prepared. After all, there's strength in numbers, and by surrounding yourself with well-prepped people, you are adding to your own preparedness. A lot of peppers follow this mindset, and actively work to recruit their neighbors into their "survival team".

There are many benefits:

Varied skill sets - We can't all be gardeners, welders, plumbers, hunters and doctors. By drawing upon the skills of your group, you have a more diverse set of skills to take advantage of.

More protection - You might have an amazing arsenal of weapons, but if it's just you and the spouse to fire them, their utility is limited. Plus, you both have to sleep sometime.

More resources - Even if your neighbors haven't loaded up on food, water and medicine, they still have a lot of resources. Additional tools, fuel, vehicles, radios, and guns are always helpful. And you never know what info or opportunities they have access to. One of them could have a relative with critical info, or be able to offer a safe harbor outside of the crisis area.

However, there's another scenario to consider.

What if you go around, preaching the gospel of being prepared, only to have it fall on deaf ears? So now, you haven't added to your own preparedness, you have in fact weakened it, because each person you spoke to knows where to go for supplies. And hungry people have a way of expecting others to bail them out of their own lack of planning.

So, what to do? I recommend a hybrid approach. Get to know your neighbors. Try to go a little beyond the smile and nod as you mow the grass. Chat with them enough to be friendly, but do not discuss prepping. Not even a little bit.

This lays a good foundation for you later. You'll be on good terms with everyone around you. You're part of the community fabric, and people's default position toward you will be positive. Additionally, you'll know a bit about them too. Do they seem resourceful? Easily stressed? The more you know, the better.

And if the dreaded moment does come? If you've done your planning, and they haven't? What do you do if a neighbor finds out you have food, and knocks on your door, asking or demanding for some?

Such a moment is not the time to start winging it. Turning them away empty-handed will sour relations fast, and you don't need to add another concern to your life at that point. In fact, it could snowball, with others joining the chorus of "hoarder" on your front porch.

Before anything else,
preparation is the key to success.
—Alexander Graham Bell

Why not plan for this situation, just like any other crisis? One relatively easy solution is to stock a little extra of the staples, like white rice, beans and lentils. In bulk, these foods are cheap, store well, and offer solid nutrition. Allocate a portion for giving away or trading. While handing out MREs would raise eyebrows, and encourage even more demands, sharing some rice won't stand out as unusual.

After all, no one needs to know that your family is eating better than that.

YOUR FINANCES

Warning! Herein lie the Non-Sexy Preps. Hey, it can't all be gear and guns.

In broad terms, I think of being prepared as taking care of my family's health and wealth. Most of the chapters up to now have covered the health angle, so let's take a look at the wealth side of things.

Car Care

You know how important your car is. In the event of an emergency, having reliable transportation could be a life-or-death situation. Do the basics now to keep your car ready to serve.

Tire Tread: Having low tread is especially dangerous when driving in wet, flood-like, snowy or icy conditions. Check the tread depth by sticking an upside down penny, with Lincoln's head toward you, into the tread. If you can see the top of his head, it's time for new tires. Every 5000 miles, have them rotated.

Tire Pressure: Once a month, check the pressure when they're still cold. Compare to the PSI number located on the driver door.

Fluids: Once a month, top off fluids like oil, coolant and wiper washer fluid. Change the oil at regular intervals. Flush the cooling system and change coolant once a year. A 50/50 mix of coolant and distilled water will keep the cooling system in good shape and prevent corrosion and deposits from building up inside the cooling system.

Belts: A broken engine belt will bring your bug-out to a sudden halt. Check for signs of fraying or wear.

Brakes: Once a year, have a technician inspect your brakes. Be aware of any signs of trouble, like noise, pulling or vibration while braking.

Battery: If your battery is older than three years, it may need to be replaced. A technician can test if it's charging at the correct rate. Be aware that extreme heat or cold can wear a battery out faster.

Have A Will

It's not fun to face your own mortality, but taking care of those we leave behind is worth it. If the costs are a concern, new services like http://legalzoom.com can do a good job with simple wills, and are very affordable.

Have Good Insurance

Home/Renter: If you own your home, you already have home insurance. If not, take a look at Renter's Insurance. It's cheap, and can replace your belongings after a disaster.

Flood: If you live in an area with flood potential, you'll want to know your options on this, although the costs are going up in many areas.

Critical Illness: If you are diagnosed with a serious illness, you may not be able to provide for your family at the same level as before. Not to mention the chance of crippling medical expenses. Critical Illness Insurance pays you a lump sum to alleviate these worries.

Typical conditions covered include : Alzheimer's disease, blindness, deafness, kidney failure, major organ transplant, multiple sclerosis, HIV/AIDS contracted by blood transfusion or during an operation, Parkinson's disease, paralysis of limb, or a terminal illness.

Life Insurance: In case of your death, will your family be taken of? This is an easy one, since for heathy people, it's quite cheap to acquire coverage. I like knowing that should something happen to me, my wife and kids won't have to worry about money for a long time.

Fire-Proof Safe

You know that collection of important papers, like birth certificates, marriage license, passports, etc? Those are difficult to replace, so why not store them inside a small fire-rated lockbox?

Fires tend to move through a home, so 30 minutes protection is generally sufficient. Check the product rating for how hot the contents might get. If you're storing papers, 350 degrees should be the maximum. If you want to store old cassette recordings or slides, you want a rating of 150 degrees or less. Computer disks and DVDs are even more sensitive, at 125 degrees.

Flash Drive

In the event of a bug-out, you will absolutely want to have a flash drive with you that contains digital copies of all important paperwork.

Imagine if you had been one of those affected by hurricane Katrina. You managed to escape the storm itself, and got yourself and family to safety. But now, a whole new struggle begins, one many people fail to anticipate: getting back on your feet.

Once the primary emergency has passed, and your health is stable, then it's time to maintain your wealth. That means recovering what assets you can, getting an income source up and running, and taking care of your various financial obligations. Having a cache of all the data that encompasses you in today's society will be a huge boon.

Some items to include:

Personal ID: Drivers licenses, Social Security cards, Birth certificates, Passports, Marriage certificate, credit cards (front and back)

Important documents: Health/auto/home insurance, Mortgage info, Car title, Utility bills, Wills, Voided check

Contact List: Family members, insurance company/account info, FEMA, Red Cross, Mortgage company, Unemployment, USPS

Pictures of your stuff: As you begin to piece your lives back together, you reach out to your insurance company, eager to get a claim started. What will you say when they ask for proof of all the furniture, clothes, electronics and valuables you claim to have lost? Maybe you could scrounge up a few receipts for the big-ticket items, but who keeps receipts for clothes?

Maybe insurance companies do this to save money, maybe to protect themselves from fraud, but either way, you don't want to get caught in that situation. Take ten minutes and go through your house, snapping pictures of everything. Your home exterior, your car, the wife's jewelry case, your closets full of clothes, the works. With 20-30 pictures, you can give a decent accounting of your belongings.

Resume: If you've relocated, it may be a good while before you can return home. Maybe your home needs to be rebuilt, so you're staying with family in another city. Getting a source of income flowing again is going to be critical. It sure would be nice to have your resume handy.

12 PROJECTS

Wondering what to do this weekend? Got you covered:

Stock a medical kit for your home. How about one for your car?

Explore your area, and learn some navigation skills by geocaching. Visit www.geocaching.com for info.

Plant a raised bed garden, and learn what grows well in your part of the world.

Build a rainwater storage system. See the previous section on Water for info.

Practice fire making with a ferro rod.

Bushcraft cooking! Cook a meal over an open fire.

Turn off your water and power, and pretend you have no gas. Limit yourself to a gallon per person per day, and see what you learn.

Luck is where opportunity meets preparation.
—Denzel Washington

Throw your bugout bag over your shoulder and go take a hike.

Go fishing. Could you feed yourself with what you catch?

Make a list of possible emergency situations, and what your plan of action will be for each.

Get your ham radio license.

Buy a compass and topographical map of your area, then learn how to navigate in a familiar area.

EVACUATION PLAN

Depending on the emergency, you may have plenty of warning, or you may have only minutes to evacuate your home.

Either way, it's smart to have a checklist prepared ahead of time. When the time comes that you need it, things will be intense, and you won't be doing your best analytical thinking. In fact, many people find that in the face of a crisis, their mind's focus shrinks and their ability to process rapidly changing events falls off dramatically. Better to refer to a list you made when things were boringly normal, and rely on your judgement made then.

I break my list down into four components, depending on how quickly we need to flee: 1 minute warning, 1 hour warning, or 6 hour warning. And what do we do once we're away and safe?

By running down the appropriate list, I can be confident we've covered what we need to, without wasting time trying to figure things out on the fly.

You may want to have your list laminated and keep it handy with your gear. Office supply stores like Staples can do the job cheaply.

ONE MINUTE WARNING

Load Bugout Bags
Load Evacuation Bag
Get out of Dodge!

ONE HOUR WARNING

Load Bugout Bags
Load Evacuation Bag
Load Medical Bag
Load Weapons
Load Fireproof Box
Load Laptop Bag
Load Fuel
Load Water/Food
Load Personal Items

SECURE HOUSE
Lock doors

Refuel car?
Get cash?

SIX HOURS WARNING

Load Bugout Bags
Load Evacuation Bag
Load Medical Bag
Load Weapons
Load Fireproof Box
Load Laptop Bag
Load Fuel
Load Water/Food
Load Personal Items
Load Car Fluids
Check Tire Pressure
Clean Car Windows

SECURE HOUSE
Lock doors
Lock windows
Adjust thermostat
Unplug lights/appliances
Turn off utilities
Prep fridge
Prep freezer/kill icemaker

Refuel car
Get cash

www.prepologyHQ.com/evac
A printable PDF of this evacuation checklist.

ONCE SAFE

Call family/friends
Contact Red Cross
Contact FEMA, get disaster ID, apply for help
Begin Unemployment
Call mortgage company for deferment
Call credit cards for deferment
Call insurance company
Change mailing address with USPS
Give everyone helpful tasks to do

Leaving The House

If you're leaving your house, an often overlooked task is to prep your fridge and freezer. Many residents of New Orleans fled in the face of Katrina, and returned to find the loss of power had effectively turned their refrigerators into unsafe and unusable petri dishes. For a time, it wasn't uncommon to see abandoned fridges, sealed shut with duct tape, set out on the curb to be hauled away as garbage.

What you want to do is this: go ahead and toss the highly perishable items. Next, take everything remaining and put it all inside heavy-duty trash bags, then put the bags back in the fridge. Do the same for your freezer. Finally, set a bowl of water in the freezer. Once it freezes solid, put a coin on top of the ice.

Close the fridge up, and head out. When you return, check the coin. If you lost power and the ice melted, it will be at the bottom of the bowl. In that case, take your neatly prepared bags of now-spoiled food and toss them out.

In case of a long power outage, this simple prep will save you a lot of time and hassle.

FAREWELL...

I hope this book has given you a solid introduction to prepping. Ideally, you now have enough knowledge to put your own plan into practice, and begin securing your future.

As for me, I'm beginning work on a new book dedicated to building the perfect Bugout Bag and Evacuation Bag. It's a huge topic, and one that really needs its own book to cover fully. If you'd like to know when it's ready, join my mailing list. I send out news and articles that I think you'd want to know about, and I'll also let you know when the new book is done. Sign up at http://prepologyHQ.com/newsletter.

Doing the research for this book has been a lot of fun, but it's also rewarding to know that it benefits others. I've heard great stories from readers about how they banished procrastination and used this book to get started in the preparedness work they always wanted to do, but didn't know to begin. If this book has motivated you, let me know! I'd love to hear from you.

Just drop me a note at chris@prepologyHQ.com.

Have fun out there, and be safe!

www.ingramcontent.com/pod-product-compliance
Lightning Source LLC
Chambersburg PA
CBHW070750290526
45795CB00002B/548